STANTON V. ARMSTRONG

STANTON V. ARMSTRONG

Elizabeth I. Boals

Associate Director
Stephen S. Weinstein Trial Advocacy Program
Washington College of Law
American University

with

Shailee Diwanji Sharma

Covington & Burling, LLP

NATIONAL INSTITUTE FOR TRIAL ADVOCACY

Address inquiries to:

Reprint Permission
National Institute for Trial Advocacy
1685 38th Street, Suite 200
Boulder, CO 80301-2735
Phone: (800) 225-6482
Fax: (720) 890-7069
Email: permissions@nita.org

ISBN 978-1-60156-581-5
eISBN 978-1-60156-582-2
FBA 1581

Printed in the United States of America

CONTENTS

DEPOSITION TRANSCRIPTS

APPENDICES

ACKNOWLEDGEMENTS

The authors would like to acknowledge the special contributions by former American University Washington College of Law (WCL) students, Annie Berry and Montra Martin, for assisting with editing and the creation of exhibits for this case file. Thanks also to Kim Green, Program Coordinator for the WCL Trial Advocacy Program, and Mary Ippolito, Senior Administrative Assistant, for their careful editing.

The National Institute for Trial Advocacy wishes to thank Twitter for its permission to use likenesses of its website as part of these teaching materials.

The National Institute for Trial Advocacy also wishes to thank YouTube for its permission to use likenesses of its website as part of these teaching materials.

CASE SUMMARY

Stanton v. Armstrong is a civil action for defamation and tortious interference with contract, brought by Harper Stanton against Toby Armstrong in the United States District Court, District of Nita. Armstrong posted the allegedly defamatory statement on July 5, YR-1 at Pageant Tips Blog. At the time of the allegedly defamatory blog post, Stanton was the Chief Executive Officer ("CEO") of Miss Olympia, Inc. and Armstrong was a blogger and the owner of a pageant contestant coaching company. Armstrong also coached a pageant contestant in the YR-1 Miss Olympia Pageant.

In the blog post at issue in this case, Armstrong wrote, "[S]teer clear of the Miss Olympia Pageant for now! An insider revealed that the runner-up made it as far as she did through a payoff to Miss Olympia's CEO. It explains how a contestant who can't answer a simple question could make it into the top five let alone end up as the runner-up. What a sham and a shame! With all the negative publicity the pageant got this year, hopefully Miss Olympia will terminate its contract with Harper Stanton and hire a new CEO!" Armstrong claims that this allegation of pageant fixing was based on information received from Stanton's former employee, Rory Carter, who reported to him that Stanton had accepted a shoebox full of money from a pageant contestant's coach, Lucy Madrid, and that during the exchange Stanton said, "Great, it looks like it's all here. Don't worry. I'll take care of you."

As a result of this blog post, Stanton claims loss of reputation and inducement for Stanton's employer, Miss Olympia, Inc., to breach its employment contract with Stanton by firing Stanton on August 15, YR-1. Stanton is currently unemployed and is seeking monetary damages.

At the YR-1 Miss Olympia Pageant, there were a number of facilities and technology malfunctions that impacted the quality of the event. Additionally, one of the judges was unable to make the event. As a result, Stanton as CEO of the YR-1 Miss Olympia Pageant and Hawkins as the Chief Judge of the pageant agreed to double Hawkins' scores to make up for the missing judge. The scoring criteria, scores, and some video footage from the YR-1 Miss Olympia Pageant are available to assist in assessing whether the pageant was, in fact, fixed.

Special Instructions for Use as a Full Trial

1. The plaintiff and the defendant must call the two witnesses listed as that party's witnesses on the witness list.

2. All witnesses are gender neutral and can be played by either a man or a woman.

3. All witnesses called to testify who have identified the parties, other individuals, or tangible evidence in statements or prior deposition testimony must, if asked, identify the same at trial. Additionally, witnesses have knowledge of all documents on which their signatures appear.

4. Each witness who testified previously agreed under oath at the outset of his or her testimony to give a full and complete description of all material events that occurred and to correct the transcript of such testimony for inaccuracies and completeness before signing the deposition transcript.

5. All exhibits in the case file are authentic. In addition, each exhibit contained in the file is the original of that document unless otherwise noted on the exhibit or as established by the evidence.

6. All signatures are authentic. No advocate may attempt to impeach a witness by arguing that a signature on a transcript, statement, or exhibit does not comport with a signature or initials on an exhibit.

7. Other than what is supplied in the problem itself, there is nothing exceptional or unusual about the background information of any of the witnesses that would bolster or detract from their credibility.

8. The case file is a "closed universe" of facts, and advocates may use only the materials in the file except where the file states otherwise.

9. "Beyond the record" shall not be entertained as an objection. Rather, advocates shall use cross-examination to impeach the witness regarding any material facts not contained in the case file. Where asked, witnesses must admit that the fact to which they have testified is not in their statement or testimony.

10. The Case Summary shall not be used as evidence or for examination or cross-examination of any witness.

Procedural Matters

11. Federal Rules of Evidence and Federal Rules of Civil Procedure apply.

12.   If the defendant is found liable, an evaluation of the damages will take place before the jury on a separate date.

13.   All dispositive pretrial motions have been filed and denied; no further dispositive motions (other than Motions for Judgment as a Matter of Law) will be entertained.

14.   The parties stipulate that Exhibits 1 through 3 accompanied the initial Verified Complaint and Jury Demand, and that they are displayed in this text in the Exhibits section solely for clarity of the layout.

SUBSTANTIVE MATTERS

15.   Stanton pursued a separate cause of action against Miss Olympia, Inc. for wrongful termination and breach of contract. That action resulted in a confidential, no-fault settlement agreement. The parties agree not to make reference to the action or settlement between Stanton and Miss Olympia, Inc.

16.   The parties stipulate that Miss Olympia, Inc. did not hire Toby Armstrong to be its Chief Executive Officer in YR-1.

17.   The parties stipulate that the individual who was scheduled to serve as the fifth judge for the YR-1 Miss Olympia Pageant was in a car accident the morning of the pageant and was unable to serve as a judge for the pageant due to injuries from the accident.

18.   The parties stipulate that following the filing of this lawsuit, the Pageant Tips Blog was taken down and is no longer publicly available on the Internet. Anticipating that this might happen, the plaintiff's counsel captured the entire site prior to filing the complaint for evidentiary purposes. The captured version is available at the microsite for evidentiary use in the courtroom, but should not be considered to have been publicly available at any time after the filing of the complaint.

19.   The parties stipulate that shortly after the YR-1 Miss Olympia Pageant, Lucy Madrid moved to China. Efforts to reach Lucy Madrid for an interview, deposition, and trial were fruitless. As a result, Lucy Madrid is unavailable to testify at trial.

20.   The parties stipulate that the 30(b)(6) deposition of Abigail Cotton, an officer from Miss Olympia, Inc., is authentic and may be read into the record, in whole or in part, by either party. This reading may be done constructively.

21.   The parties stipulate that Exhibit 17 is a true and accurate video recording excerpted from the YR-1 Miss Olympia Pageant that contains the interview question by the pageant host and complete answer given by contestant, Miss Scattersburg.

22.   The parties stipulate that Exhibit 18 is a true and accurate audio recording of an interview between Frank Pittman, Chair of the Board of Directors for Miss Olympia, Inc. and Janie Apple, radio personality at the Altamont Radio News Show, which aired on July 10, YR-1.

UNITED STATES DISTRICT COURT
DISTRICT OF NITA

HARPER STANTON,	)	
	)	
Plaintiff,	)	
	)	
vs.	)	Case No: 00-CV-5120
	)	
TOBY ARMSTRONG,	)	
	)	
Defendant.	)	
	)	

VERIFIED COMPLAINT AND JURY DEMAND

Preliminary Statement

1. This civil action is brought by Plaintiff Harper Stanton against Defendant Toby Armstrong for damages caused by Defendant's defamatory statements and tortious interference with contract on July 5, YR-1.

Jurisdiction

2. This Court has diversity jurisdiction in this case pursuant to 28 U.S.C. § 1332 because Plaintiff and Defendant are residents of different states and the amount of damages claimed exceeds $75,000.

3. Venue is proper pursuant to 28 U.S.C. § 1391(a).

Parties

4. Plaintiff Stanton is a citizen and resident of the State of Olympia.

5. Defendant Armstrong is a citizen and resident of the State of Nita.

Factual Assertions

6. Plaintiff has worked in the beauty pageant industry for over twenty years.

7. From August YR-4 to August YR-1, Plaintiff was employed by Miss Olympia, Inc. as its Chief Executive Officer ("CEO").

8. Miss Olympia, Inc. owns and annually stages the Miss Olympia Pageant for beauty pageant contestants from the State of Olympia.

9. Miss Olympia is a high-profile state pageant, and its winner represents the State of Olympia as a contestant in the annual Miss America Pageant.

10. Plaintiff's employment contract with Miss Olympia, Inc. was a five-year, renewable contract, set to expire in August YR+1. [Exhibit 1]

11. Plaintiff was paid an annual salary of $250,000 under the employment contract with Miss Olympia, Inc.

12. Plaintiff's employment with Miss Olympia, Inc. was not at-will employment.

13. Upon information and belief, Defendant owns and runs the company Pageant Stars Coaching Service.

14. According to its website, Pageant Stars Coaching Service is a full-service organization that coaches and sponsors beauty pageant contestants at beauty pageants across the country.

15. Upon information and belief, Defendant is the sole writer of Pageant Tips Blog and the blog is not affiliated with Pageant Stars Coaching Service.

16. On July 5, YR-1, Defendant published a post on Pageant Tips Blog, a public website, that stated, "[S]teer clear of the Miss Olympia Pageant for now! An insider revealed that the runner-up made it as far as she did through a payoff to Miss Olympia's CEO. That explains how a contestant who can't answer a simple question could make it into the top five let alone end up as the runner-up! What a sham and a shame! With all the negative publicity the pageant got this year, hopefully Miss Olympia will terminate its contract with Harper Stanton and hire a new CEO!" [Exhibit 2]

17. Plaintiff did not receive a payoff for the benefit of any contestant in the YR-1 Miss Olympia Pageant.

18. Plaintiff did not personally score or select any contestant in the YR-1 Miss Olympia Pageant.

19. Defendant's blog post was published on a publicly accessible website and was brought to Plaintiff's attention in an email from a friend, Missy Sussman. [Exhibit 3]

20. Plaintiff did not engage in any activity that breached Plaintiff's employment contract with Miss Olympia, Inc.

21. On August 2, YR-1, Miss Olympia, Inc. informed Plaintiff that it was terminating Plaintiff's employment contract.

22. In an interview on July 10, YR-1, the Chairman of Miss Olympia, Inc.'s board of directors made the following statement regarding the blog post [Exhibit 2] on a radio show: "Such allegations are very serious and are harmful to the reputation and the integrity of the Miss Olympia Pageant. As you can imagine, this is not a situation where any press is good press. We will act accordingly."

23. Upon information and belief, Miss Olympia, Inc. terminated Plaintiff's contract because of statements made by Defendant in the July 5, YR-1, public blog post.

Count I—Defamation

24. Defendant's blog post statements were false and defamatory toward Plaintiff.

25. Defendant's statement was one of fact, not of opinion.

26. Defendant's defamatory statement was published to third parties through Defendant's blog, Pageant Tips Blog.

33. Defendant denies the allegations in paragraph 33.

34. Defendant admits the allegations in paragraph 34.

35. Defendant lacks sufficient personal knowledge to form a belief about the truth or falsity of the allegations in paragraph 35 and therefore denies it.

<u>First Affirmative Defense to Defamation—Truth</u>

36. Defendant affirmatively asserts that all statements by Defendant about Plaintiff were true and thus cannot be the basis of a defamation action.

<u>Second Affirmative Defense to Defamation—Qualified Privilege</u>

37. Defendant's blog post is considered qualified privilege and statements within the post are protected against claims of defamation.

<u>First Affirmative Defense to Tortious Interference with Contract—</u>

<u>Fair and Reasonable Conduct</u>

38. Defendant's actions were fair and reasonable under the circumstances.

<u>Second Affirmative Defense to Defamation and Tortious Interference with Contract—</u>

<u>Lack of Damage Caused by Defendant's Statements</u>

39. No act or omission on the part of Defendant either caused or contributed to whatever injury (if any) Plaintiff is claiming.

REQUEST FOR RELIEF

WHEREFORE, Defendant respectfully requests that Plaintiff's complaint be dismissed with prejudice, that Plaintiff be ordered to pay Defendant the costs of this suit, and for any other such relief that this Court deems just and proper.

JURY DEMAND

Defendant requests that this action be tried before a jury.

Date: October 3, YR-1

Respectfully Submitted,

/s/ Zachary Allen
Zachary Allen
Allen Whitaker LLP
350 Archrival St.
Nita City, Nita

EXHIBITS

Exhibit 1

Miss Olympia, Inc.
EMPLOYMENT CONTRACT

This contract of employment is made the <u>20th</u> day of <u>July</u> YR-4, between <u>Harper Stanton</u> ("Employee") and <u>Miss Olympia, Inc.</u> ("Employer"). The regulations and conditions of employment as set out herein will be deemed to constitute a "Contract of Employment."

(i)   *Date of Commencement*: <u>1 August</u>, YR-4.

(ii)   *Job Function*: The Employee shall be employed as <u>Chief Executive Officer</u>, and he/she shall carry out all associated functions.

(iii)   *Salary*: The Employee's annual salary shall be <u>$250,000</u>. This salary is non-reviewable over the duration of this contract.

[Omitted]

[Omitted]

(xx)   *Duration of Contract*: This contract is valid for five (5) years and, at the end of that period, may be renewed by the parties if the parties so desire.

(xxi)   *Performance*: Employee must perform his/her duties to the satisfaction of Employer. Non-performance is grounds for termination of this employment agreement.

(xxii)   *Liquidated Damages*: Should this contract be breached in any way, the party in breach of this contract will owe the damaged party <u>six (6)</u> months of the salary described in paragraph (iii) of this agreement.

I agree to be bound by the regulations and conditions of employment as contained in the foregoing.

Signed:

Harper Stanton
Harper Stanton

Signed for an on behalf of Miss Olympia, Inc.:

Abigail Cotton
Abigail Cotton

Exhibit 2

Choosing the Right Pageant

Posted by Toby Armstrong on July 5, YR-1

This week I have been selected to be a guest blogger on the Puffington Post! I wanted to focus on information that I think would benefit the pageant world and bring attention to the public. With so many different pageants to choose from, how do you pick the right one for you? Here are some things for you to think about:

Title Level. Are you looking for a local, state, national, or international title? Different pageants lead you to different places.

Title Prizes. What do you hope to win? Prizes? Scholarship money? A new career opportunity? Pageants have different focuses and commitment levels, so research the pageant to be sure it aligns with your goals.

Title Reputation. Different pageants are run by different companies, each with its own reputation. Research the pageant in the news, talk to other contestants and pageant coaches before you decide to enter into a pageant. The last thing you want is for the pageant to be a disaster after all the time, effort, and money you put into preparing for it!

For instance, steer clear of the Miss Olympia Pageant for now! An insider revealed that the runner up made it as far as she did through a payoff to Miss Olympia's CEO. It explains how a contestant who can't answer a simple question could make it into the top five let alone end up as the runner up. What a sham and a shame! With all the negative publicity the pageant got this year, hopefully Miss Olympia will terminate its contract with Harper Stanton and hire a new CEO!

Money. Pageants can be expensive! Make sure you know how much competing in a particular pageant will cost, and budget accordingly.

Experience. If you are new, start with smaller pageants. This will help you build confidence, gain experience, and decide if this is something you want to pursue. Then you can move onto prime time!

The pageant world is small and the pool of qualified judges is even smaller. Your best scores will come from judges who see you compete for the first time. So choose carefully.

Share:

Google   Facebook   Twitter   More

Exhibit 3

Harper Stanton

From:	Missy Sussman (m.sussman@fashionation.nita)
Sent:	Monday, July 8, YR-1 8:05 a.m.
To:	Harper Stanton (hstant@email.nita)
Subject:	Rumor has it?

Harper,

Read a shocking rumor over the weekend. Have you seen this yet?

www.pageanttipsblog.com/choosetherightpageant.htm/

Such an awful thing to say! I know you have a history with Armstrong, but I think this crosses the line. Let me know if there's anything I can do to help.

On a side note, saw the pageant last weekend. Amazing, as always. Don't heed the media. Talkers talk.

Hang in there! Missy
Missy Sussman
Assistant Buyer—Women's Evening Attire Fashionation Department Stores

Exhibit 4

YR-2 Performance Review for Rory Carter from Miss Olympia, Inc.

Miss Olympia, Inc.

Employee Information

Employee Performance Review

Employee Name: **Rory Carter**
Job Title: **Senior Administrative Assistant**
Department: **Head Office**
Manager: **Harper Stanton**
Review Period: **11/YR-3 to 10/YR-2**

Employee ID: **21205**
Date: **October 2, YR-2**

Evaluation

Use this rating key for the following evaluation:

1 = *Unsatisfactory*
   Does not perform required tasks. Requires constant supervision
2 = *Marginal*
   Needs improvement in quality of work. Completes tasks, but not on time.
3 = *Meets Requirements*
   Meets basic requirements. Tasks are completed on time.
4 = *Exceeds Requirements*
   Goes above and beyond expectations.
5 = *Exceptional*
   Always gets results far beyond what is required.

	(5) = Exceptional	(4) = Exceeds Requirements	(3) = Meets Requirements	(2) = Marginal	(1) = Unsatisfactory
Achieves Set Objectives	X	☐	☐	☐	☐
Open to Constructive Criticism	☐	X	☐	☐	☐
Demonstrates Required Job Skills and Knowledge	X	☐	☐	☐	☐
Demonstrates Effective Management and Leadership Skills	X	☐	☐	☐	☐
Completes All Assigned Responsibilities	X	☐	☐	☐	☐
Meets Attendance Requirements	X	☐	☐	☐	☐
Takes Responsibility for Actions	X	☐	☐	☐	☐
Recognizes Potential Problems and Develops Solutions	☐	X	☐	☐	☐
Demonstrates Problem-Solving Skills	X	☐	☐	☐	☐

Offers Constructive Suggestions for Improvement	☐	X	☐	☐	☐
Generates Creative Ideas and Solutions	X	☐	☐	☐	☐
Provides Alternatives When Making Recommendations	☐	X	☐	☐	☐

Additional Comments:
None.

Provide Suggestions For Improvement:
Trust yourself. Make more suggestions for improvements to business. Be open to constructive criticism.

Supervisor/Manager Feedback:
Rory is a wonderful employee! Rory is hardworking and diligent and shows great potential for growth. I hope to see Rory in a leadership role in our company one day!

Verification of Review

By signing this form, you confirm that you have discussed this review in detail with your supervisor. Signing this form does not necessarily indicate that you agree with this evaluation.

I, *Rory Carter*, acknowledge receipt of review, and my signature does not necessarily indicate agreement.

Rory Carter	**10/2/YR-2**
Employee Signature	Date
Harper Stanton	**10/2/YR-2**
Manager Signature	Date

Exhibit 5

YR-1 Performance Review for Rory Carter from Miss Olympia, Inc.

Miss Olympia, Inc.

Employee Performance Review

Employee Information

Employee Name: **Rory Carter**   Employee ID: **21205**

Job Title: **Senior Administrative Assistant**   Date: **October 5, YR-1**

Department: **Head Office**

Manager: **Abigail Cotton, Director of Human Resources**

Review Period: **11/YR-2 to 10/YR-1**

Evaluation

Use this rating key for the following evaluation:

1 = *Unsatisfactory*
   Does not perform required tasks. Requires constant supervision
2 = *Marginal*
   Needs improvement in quality of work. Completes tasks, but not on time.
3 = *Meets Requirements*
   Meets basic requirements. Tasks are completed on time.
4 = *Exceeds Requirements*
   Goes above and beyond expectations.
5 = *Exceptional*
   Always gets results far beyond what is required.

	(5) = Exceptional	(4) = Exceeds Requirements	(3) = Meets Requirements	(2) = Marginal	(1) = Unsatisfactory
Achieves Set Objectives	☐	☐	X	☐	☐
Open to Constructive Criticism	☐	☐	X	☐	☐
Demonstrates Required Job Skills and Knowledge	☐	☐	X	☐	☐
Demonstrates Effective Management and Leadership Skills	☐	☐	☐	X	☐
Completes All Assigned Responsibilities	☐	☐	X	☐	☐
Meets Attendance Requirements	☐	X	☐	☐	☐
Takes Responsibility for Actions	☐	☐	☐	X	☐
Recognizes Potential Problems and Develops Solutions	☐	☐	X	☐	☐
Demonstrates Problem-Solving Skills	☐	☐	X	☐	☐

Offers Constructive Suggestions for Improvement	☐	☐	☐	X	☐
Generates Creative Ideas and Solutions	☐	☐	X	☐	☐
Provides Alternatives When Making Recommendations	☐	☐	X	☐	☐

Additional Comments:
None.

Provide Suggestions For Improvement:
Approach internal management with problems and seek resolution of issues through chain of command.

Supervisor/Manager Feedback:
The quality of Rory's performance has decreased this year. Rory seems less interested in the day-to-day operations of our business. Rory should refrain from discussing internal company business with outside parties. Rather, Rory should consider using the resources available to all employees for support—HR, senior management, etc. Nevertheless, Rory has potential to be a positive asset to our company but improvement is needed.

Verification of Review

By signing this form, you confirm that you have discussed this review in detail with your supervisor. Signing this form does not necessarily indicate that you agree with this evaluation.

I, *Rory Carter*, acknowledge receipt of review, and my signature does not necessarily indicate agreement.

Rory Carter	10/5/YR-1
Employee Signature	Date
Abigail Cotton	10/5/YR-1
Manager Signature	Date

Exhibit 6

Deposit slip for cash deposit to account of Harper Stanton

Deposit:

(Check One) ☒ Checking ☐ Savings ☐ Money Market Access ☐ Command

Account Number

* 50000377 Date June 30, YR-1

Please print: Name

Harper Stanton

Please print: Street Address, City, State, Zip Code

2435 Amber Av, Altamont, OY

Please sign in teller's presence for cash received Two forms of ID may be required for cash back transactions.

X Harper Stanton

Deposits may not be available for immediate withdrawal See Delayed posting information on reverse *

Cash 17200.00

Total Checks (exclude total from other side)

Subtotal 17200.00

Minus cash back

Total $ 17200.00

Bank Use Only (When SVT Is Not Available) TLR8607 (08/11) wros17 13352399

Customer Id	Exp. date	Token Verified (✓) X	Approval MM

⑈715884455⑈ ⑆50000377⑆

Exhibit 7

Toby Armstrong

From: Toby Armstrong (toby.armstrong@pageantstars.nita)
Sent: Tuesday, August 20, YR-1 3:45 p.m.
To: Ambrosia McSweeney (amcsweeney@beauterrific.nita)
Subject: Potential Employee—Rory Carter

Hi Am,

It was wonderful to see you today! It had been so long since we caught up. I can hardly believe that Ashton and Eva are teenagers already. Next time bring pictures—I bet they look so grown up!

As I mentioned over lunch today, there's a kid you should hire. Rory Carter. Rory will be putting in an application soon. You should take the application seriously. Worth hiring. Really hard worker and a bit of a goody two-shoes. That's not a bad thing in our industry! Rory was mentored personally by Harper Stanton, but don't reject the application just for that small flaw. Rory was the one who helped me unveil the corruption ring at Miss Olympia. But the kid's scared to death about employment ramifications—apparently Abigail Cotton, the HR Director over at Miss Olympia, is supervising Rory now, and it's not going well. I'm not surprised, she has a reputation—keep this on the down-low, but I heard Abigail's the one who Stanton cheated with! Anyway, do me a favor and help me out here. I'll vouch for the kid, and I'll even owe you one.

Don't be a stranger,
Toby

Toby Armstrong
7210 Prometheus Circle
Suite 300
Washingtonia
(303) 555-9280
toby.armstrong@pageantstars.nita

Exhibit 8

YR-1 Miss Olympia Pageant Master Score Sheet

Miss Olympia Pageant
YR-1 Master Score Sheet

	A		Swimsuit					Evening Wear					Talent					Interview				
			H	P	B	W	X	H	P	B	W	X	H	P	B	W	X	H	P	B	W	X
W	9.9	Ms. Winnerton	10	10	10	10	10	10	10	10	9	10	10	9	10	10	10	10	10	10	10	10
R1	9.1	Ms. Scattersburg	10	10	10	10	10	10	10	10	10	10	10	8	8	8	10	9	7	6	6	9
R2	9	Ms. Newbury	10	10	10	10	10	9	8	10	9	9	8	9	9	8	8	8	9	9	9	8
T5	8.9	Ms. Napapolis	9	9	10	9	9	8	9	10	9	8	9	10	9	8	9	9	9	8	8	9
T5	8.8	Ms. Brightfax	9	9	9	9	9	9	8	9	8	9	9	9	10	9	9	8	9	8	8	8
T10	8.6	Ms. Sphinx	10	9	9	9	10	8	8	8	9	8	8	9	7	9	8	-	-	-	-	-
T10	8.3	Ms. Doryville	9	9	8	9	9	8	9	9	9	8	8	7	7	8	8	-	-	-	-	-
T10	7.9	Ms. Bethburg	9	8	8	8	9	8	9	8	8	8	7	7	7	8	7	-	-	-	-	-
T10	7.3	Ms. Frenchtown	8	8	8	9	8	8	8	9	8	8	5	6	5	6	5	-	-	-	-	-
T10	7.3	Ms. Gold Spring	9	8	8	8	9	7	8	9	6	7	6	6	7	6	6	-	-	-	-	-

[Scores for the remaining contestants have been redacted for brevity]

Key A = Average; H = Judge Hawkins; P = Judge Preska; B = Judge Buchwald; W = Judge Wood; X = Missing
Judge

W = Winner; R1 = First Runner-Up; R2 = Second Runner-Up; T5 = Top Five; T10 = Top Ten

Note The scores of the chief judge were duplicated for the missing judge.

This document was prepared on June 30, YR-1, by Farber & Associates on behalf of Miss Olympia, Inc.

Exhibit 9

Map of Harper Stanton's office

HARPER STANTON'S OFFICE

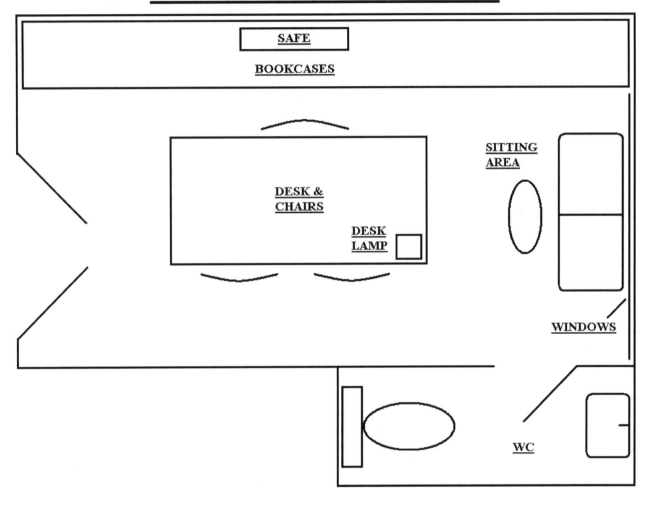

Exhibit 10

Taylor Hawkins

From: Harper Stanton (hstant@email.nita)
Sent: Thursday, February 21, YR-1 10:23 a.m.
To: Taylor Hawkins (taylorhawk@outlook.nita)
Subject: Re: YR-1 Pageant

Taylor,

Next time please email me about this stuff on my personal account.

You can put down June 30th on your calendar. I personally guarantee that you will be at our pageant as a judge. In fact, as we discussed a few months ago, we'll have you be the chief judge at the pageant this year. You have been a fair and consistent judge, a benefactor of the pageant, and a personal friend for a long time now, so this is the least I can do for you. And, frankly, your experience and your loyalty recommend you well for the post.

By the way, I put another package in the mail for you today. You should receive it in a couple of days. It has some good stuff—I hope there's enough there to keep you interested in our deal.

Looking forward to seeing you at the benefit gala next week. Harper

Exhibit 11

Scoring Sheet Instructions

Each contestant is competing against herself and receives a score in the 1 to 10 point range, in whole numbers, for all categories. More than one contestant may receive the same score.

Scoring Criteria

- **Swimsuit**—A contestant will be assessed on the following criteria:
  - Overall "First Impression"
  - Attractiveness and Presence
  - Lifestyle Statement of Strong Physical Health—is the contestant fit?
  - Walk, Posture, Carriage, and Grace
  - Sense of Confidence and Composure
  - Displays Energy, Charisma, and Expression

- **Evening Wear**—A contestant will be assessed on the following criteria:
  - Overall "First Impression"
  - Sense of Confidence
  - Stage Presence—does she command the stage?
  - Walk, Posture, Carriage, and Grace
  - Sense of Style and Appropriateness of the Evening Wear
  - Beauty, Attractiveness, and Charm

- **Talent; Top Ten**—A contestant will be assessed on the following criteria:
  - Selection and Performance—demonstrates personality and skill
  - Interpretive Ability and Technical Skill Level—execution and technique
  - Stage Presence—on-stage personality
  - Costume, Props, Music, Voice, and Choreography

- Audience Enjoyment of the Presentation
- Synchronization and Control

- **Interview; Top Five**—A contestant will be assessed on the following criteria:
  - Knowledge and Understanding of Questions
  - Confident and Commanding Presence
  - Personality, Appearance, and Attractiveness
  - Supported Opinions and Responses
  - Exceptional Communication Skills—speech, vocabulary, and diction

Exhibit 12

July 23, YR-4

[**VIA** Email and First Class Mail]
Toby Armstrong
Pageant Stars Coaching Service
185 Beaumont Avenue
Nita City, Nita

RE: Chief Executive Officer Dear Toby:

It is with the deepest regrets that we inform you that we are unable to offer you the position of Chief Executive Officer of Miss Olympia, Inc. Unfortunately, the board has decided to hire someone with more pageant management experience at this time.

The response we received to our job posting was overwhelming—from nearly 300 applications, we interviewed four individuals. As one of our selected interviewees, you must know that we think very highly of your qualifications and credentials. In fact, the board thoroughly enjoyed meeting you and hearing your many anecdotes from the pageant industry.

We strongly encourage you to reapply if the position opens again in the future. We are always looking for individuals of your caliber to join our team. In the meantime, should you have any questions or concerns, please reach out to our Director of Human Resources, Abigail Cotton at abicotton@missolympia.nita.

Very truly yours,

Frank B. Pittman

Frank B. Pittman
Chairman, Board of Directors
Miss Olympia, Inc.

9800 Armante Road, Altamont, OL (630) 555-2125 | (630) 555-2120
generalinquiry@missolympia.nita | www.missolympia.nita

Exhibit 13

Picture of the bathroom door in Stanton's Office

Exhibit 14

UNITED STATES DISTRICT COURT
DISTRICT OF NITA

HARPER STANTON,	)	
	)	
Plaintiff,	)	
	)	
vs.	)	Case No: 00-CV-5120
	)	
	)	
TOBY ARMSTRONG,	)	
	)	
Defendant.	)	
	)	

NOTICE OF F.R.C.P. 30(b)(6) DEPOSITION OF MISS OLYMPIA, INC.

PLEASE TAKE NOTICE that, pursuant to Federal Rule of Civil Procedure 30(b)(6), Defendant in the above action, Toby Armstrong, hereby notices the deposition of Miss Olympia, Inc. as an organization on the topics detailed below. Defendant provides notice to Miss Olympia, Inc. and other parties to this action that the deposition may be used at the time of trial. Miss Olympia, Inc. shall identify the persons who will speak on its behalf on each topic below at least seven days before the deposition(s).

DATE OF DEPOSITION: December 6, YR-1
LOCATION OF DEPOSITION: Allen Whitaker LLP
                                                                       350 Archrival St.
                                                                       Nita City, Nita

You are advised that you must designate one or more officers, directors, managing agents, or other persons who will testify on your behalf regarding the matters listed in schedule A which are known or reasonably available to Miss Olympia, Inc.

SCHEDULE A

1. The application and interview process for the position of Chief Executive Officer as it took place in YR-4, including but not limited to, the individual or group of individuals conducting the interviews, the decision-making process, and letters of rejection sent to candidates, particularly Defendant Toby Armstrong.

2. Rory Carter's performance at the company, including performance evaluations for YR-2 and YR-1.

3. YR-1 Miss Olympia pageant, including but not limited to, events surrounding the actual pageant and any news stories emanating from the pageant.

4. Allegations of pageant-fixing against Harper Stanton, as well as comments made to the press and remedial actions taken.

5. Harper Stanton's employment contract and the events surrounding the termination of that contract.

DATED: November 17, YR-1

Respectfully submitted,

Zachary Allen
Zachary Allen
Allen Whitaker LLP
350 Archrival St.
Nita City, Nita

Exhibit 15

The Daily Post

July 1, YR-1

Miss Olympia Pageant Goes Awry . . . Again?

by Ashley Parker

ALTAMONT—The Royal Casino hosted the sixty-third Miss Olympia Pageant last night, but the show was less than royal. After we vocalized our disappointment at last year's Miss Olympia Pageant, we did not expect to be disappointed again. The generally reputable pageant ran into a string of disasters . . . this time much worse than last year. The episode left viewers wondering if they had been watching the pageant or a real-life blooper reel.

It began with an uncharacteristically late start. The 7:00 p.m. pageant began at 7:35 p.m. instead—a folly that might be easily overlooked, except the emcee's microphone stopped working on at least three different occasions (yes, we were counting!), and the air-conditioning cut off halfway through the production. This was a hot competition, but not in a good way!

Not to be outdone, the contestants too had some bloopers. Miss Stoneville stumbled on her six-inch heels and almost collided into a row of contestants during the swimsuit competition. And when Miss Frenchtown's music cut out in the middle of her talent number, she continued dancing for what seemed like an eternity without any music. As we have come to expect from these pageants, we had at least one contestant completely mis-answer the judges' question, but still end up in second place.

We certainly hope the pageant blooper reel was an aberration rather than the new normal. Though, admittedly, we'll be watching anyway!

NOTE: Miss Olympia officials have declined to comment.

Exhibit 16

STATE OF OLYMPIA
COURT OF COMMON PLEAS
DIVISION OF DOMESTIC RELATIONS

IMOGENE STANTON,   )
)

Plaintiff,   )
)

vs.   )   Case No: 13-MG-4510
)

)

HARPER STANTON,   )
)

Defendant.   )
)

DECREE OF DIVORCE

This cause came to be heard on May 13, YR-1, on the Complaint of Imogene Stanton. The Court finds that there has been service of summons as provided by law, that Plaintiff Imogene Stanton and Defendant Harper Stanton appeared personally at the hearing, that Plaintiff was represented by counsel and Defendant was represented by counsel.

The Court finds that Plaintiff has been a resident of the State of Olympia for at least six (6) months immediately prior to the filing of the Complaint on October 12, YR-2, and the Court has full and complete jurisdiction to determine the case.

The parties were married in Fairfield, Olympia, in YR-21, and there were two children born issue of their marriage: Sally and Michael.

The Court finds that the parties have irreconcilable differences and that Plaintiff is entitled to a divorce as prayed for in the Complaint.

IT IS THEREFORE ORDERED, ADJUDGED AND DECREED by the Court that a Decree of Divorce is hereby granted to the Plaintiff, and the marriage relationship existing between the parties is hereby terminated and held for naught and both parties are hereby released and discharged from all obligations thereon.

IT IS FURTHER ORDERED that Imogene Stanton is the residential parent and legal custodian of the minor child, Michael, and Harper Stanton shall have parenting time with the minor child in accordance with the Court's Standard Parenting Order, a copy of which is attached hereto.

Michael Donovan
Judge

Imogene Stanton
Plaintiff

Harper Stanton
Defendant

Exhibit 17

Video clip of interview question for Miss Scattersburg, YR-1 Miss Olympia Runner up

See clip at http://bit.ly/1P20Jea
Password: Stanton1

Exhibit 18

Audio clip of radio interview with Miss Olympia Chairman of the Board, Frank Pittman

See clip at http://bit.ly/1P20Jea
Password: Stanton1

Exhibit 19

TRANSCRIPT OF MEDIA INTERVIEW OF MR. PITTMAN, CHAIRMAN OF THE MISS OLYMPIA, INC. BOARD OF DIRECTORS

Date: July 10, YR-1

Reporter: We are joined today by Mr. Frank Pittman, Chairman of the Miss Olympia Inc. board of directors. Thank you so much, Mr. Pittman, for joining us today. Congratulations on completing the YR-1 Pageant.

PITTMAN: Thank you. Thank you. We are now looking forward to next year's pageant.

Reporter: Wow! You hardly get a breath. Were you pleased with how this year's Miss Olympia pageant turned out?

PITTMAN: Well, things could have gone better, but then again, things can always go better.

Reporter: I know exactly how you feel. So, let me ask you, have you read the blog post alleging that your pageant this year was fixed?

PITTMAN: Unfortunately, yes, I have read that post.

Reporter: How did you hear about the post?

PITTMAN: The post is known within the pageant world. A few industry insiders read it in connection with larger websites that discuss pageant matters.

Reporter: Well, the post refers to an insider. Can you tell us who that insider is?

PITTMAN: Honestly, at this time, I cannot comment on that.

Reporter: So, can you tell us anything?

PITTMAN: Such allegations are very serious and are harmful to the reputation and the integrity of the Miss Olympia Pageant. As you can imagine, this is not a situation where any press is good press. We will act accordingly.

Reporter: Thank you for your time, Mr. Pittman.

PITTMAN: You're welcome.

[End]

Exhibit 20

Blog post from Pageant Tips Blog, dated April 3, YR-1

Welcome!

Posted by Toby Armstrong on April 3, YR-1

Fabulous to-be contestants,

Welcome to my latest venture, Toby Armstrong's pageant blog! Here I will share with you tips, tricks, and industry secrets. But shhh, don't tell anyone!

Before I tell you a bit about pageants, let me tell you about myself. I am Toby Armstrong, and I have been working in the pageant industry for over fifteen years! If there is something to know about the pageant industry, trust me, I know it. For the last several years, I have been running the Pageant Stars Coaching Service, a full service coaching organization for beauty pageant contestants. If you are getting ready to participate in a high profile city or state pageant, a coaching service is a must! With our Pageant Stars Coaching Service, you can have an expert with you every step of the way!

Pageants transform girls into young women, setting them up for a successful future. Although people criticize pageants for objectifying women, that notion is far from the truth. Today, many young women compete in pageants to win scholarships for further education, to be a role model for young girls around the world, and to help make a difference through community service work. These young women learn to carry themselves well, to engage in conversation, and to connect with people. They truly emerge confident, beautiful young women, ready to take on any challenge the world throws their way.

On this blog I will also be sharing information about the pageant world at large and giving you ways to be safe and informed. There are so many shady things that go on and I want to share what I know to keep contestants in the know!

Participating in a pageant? Follow me on this blog, and I will tell you everything you need to know!

Share:

Exhibit 22

Blog post from Pageant Tips Blog, dated August 3, YR-1

Pageant Posture

Posted by Toby Armstrong on August 3, YR-1

If your mom was anything like mine, she probably told you and told you often to stand up straight. Surprise, surprise ladies—she was right!

Imagine this. This is your first pageant. Things have been going great, and it's time for your very first stage solo. You walk out onto the stage, and the spotlight hits you. Do you want to be hunched over and closed up? Or would you rather be the showstopper?!

Well, if you would rather be the showstopper, think long, lean, and leggy! And it all starts with good posture.

Here are a couple of great little exercises to help you on your way to better posture:

<u>Shoulder rolls</u>. Stand in a comfortable position with your arms by your side. Raise your shoulders and shoulder blades to your ears. Hold. Then pull your shoulder blades down and together. Repeat five times.

<u>Pyramid</u>. Stand with your feet shoulder width apart. Step your left foot back so it rests fully on the floor; both feet face forward. Square your hips. Clasp your forearms behind your back and lean forward from your hips. Be sure to keep you spine straight. Count to five and rise. Switch sides.

<u>Chair Pose</u>. Stand and raise your arms in front of you to shoulder height. Contract your arm muscles. Bend your knees (no more than 90 degrees), keeping them over your toes. Count to five and then stand. Repeat five times.

You only get to make a first impression once—so stand tall and make the right first impression!

Share:

Google   Facebook   Twitter   More

Deposition Transcripts

UNITED STATES DISTRICT COURT
DISTRICT OF NITA

HARPER STANTON,

Plaintiff,

vs.   Case No: 00-CV-5120

TOBY ARMSTRONG,

Defendant.

DEPOSITION TESTIMONY

<u>HARPER STANTON</u>, having been first duly sworn, was examined and testified as follows:

EXAMINATION

<u>By ZACHARY ALLEN, Attorney for the Defendant</u>:

Q. Please state your name for the record.

A. My name is Harper Stanton.

Q. Where do you live?

A. I live at 3720 Applewood Lane, Apt 15D, Fairfield, Olympia.

Q. How old are you?

A. I am fifty-seven years old.

Q. Are you married?

A. I've been divorced for less than a year.

Q. Do you have any children?

A. Two. A son in eleventh grade, and a daughter who's a senior in college.

Q. Did you go to college?

A. Yes, I did.

Q. What did you study?

A. I studied business management and fashion technology at the University of Olympia.

Q. What did you do after you graduated from the University of Olympia?

A. I worked in the fashion and pageant industries. If you want me to go through my resume, we'll be here a while.

Q. No, that'll suffice. Did you ever work at Beauterrific, Inc.?

A. Yes, from about YR-19 to YR-10.

Q. What was your role at Beauterrific?

A. I was the Chief Pageant Director.

Q. Where did you work after you left Beauterrific in YR-10?

A. I became the CEO of the Fairfield Beauty Pageant. I had worked on bigger pageants at Beauterrific, so this was a bit of a step down. But Fairfield had just launched its pageant and needed some experienced hands to guide it. In the six years that I was there, I took the Fairfield Beauty Pageant from fifteen participants to fifty participants, and from a deficit to a yearly gross revenue of over $2 million.

Q. Why did you leave the Fairfield Pageant?

A. Well, I got a much bigger opportunity to run the Miss Olympia Pageant.

Q. When did you join Miss Olympia?

A. In YR-4.

Q. I am showing you what has been marked as Exhibit 1. Do you recognize it?

A. Yes. This is my employment contract with Miss Olympia, Inc.

Q. Do you still work there?

A. Are you serious? You know I don't. I was fired on August 2, YR-1. I knew when I saw that blog post there was going to be trouble.

Q. What blog post are you referring to?

A. The one we are here about, of course. The one written by Armstrong about how to choose a pageant.

Q. How did you come across this blog post?

A. A friend emailed me a link. Before I received the link, I had never even heard of Armstrong's stupid little blog. I couldn't believe it when I saw it.

Q. What do you do now?

A. I'm taking a sabbatical. After the divorce and all this drama, I need some time to rejuvenate.

Q. Do you know Toby Armstrong?

A. Unfortunately, yes. We worked together at Beauterrific. And since Armstrong's now a coach, we cross paths from time to time.

Q. What was your relationship with Armstrong at Beauterrific?

A. I supervised Armstrong in various roles at Beauterrific. Armstrong was a really hard worker, but not a team player at all. In fact, that's what cost Armstrong a key promotion at Beauterrific.

Armstrong has a hard time being happy for other people. For instance, the first time I saw Armstrong after I'd been appointed CEO of Miss Olympia, I thought I'd share the news of my new job and how excited I was about it, and Armstrong just reacted with jealousy and said I was just trying to rub it in. Until then, I hadn't even realized Armstrong had also applied for the job. Honestly, Armstrong has never liked me.

Q. Do you know Rory Carter?

A. Yes, Carter was my personal aide at Miss Olympia. Carter wasn't the best or smartest employee by any means, but Carter showed up every day and did what I asked. I thought Carter was honest and trustworthy, but obviously, I was very mistaken.

Q. Why do you say you were mistaken?

A. Well, the obvious reason is the rumor Carter set in motion. It completely snowballed, and I lost my job as a result of it. Carter's biggest mistake was going to Toby Armstrong, who will stop at nothing to fulfill a personal vendetta against me. And ultimately, it was Armstrong's blog post that cost me my job.

Q. Are there other reasons?

A. Unfortunately, yes. I would have been likely to forgive Carter's idiocy as the folly of youth, but now I know Carter's also a liar. Carter made up the whole thing about looking through the window above the bathroom door, the transom, and seeing my exchange with Lucy Madrid. The transom is translucent, except for the small stars, and contrary to what Carter says, it wasn't open. So Carter couldn't have seen what was in the box and just made up a story about seeing money. Carter also claims the office was flooded with light. Well, I don't see how that's possible. I'm obsessed with privacy, so the blinds in my office are always closed. Always. The only light in the room is from a small desk lamp that I have.

Q. I'm showing you Exhibit 9. Do you recognize it?

A. Yes, I do. It's a map of my office.

Q. Is it a fair and accurate copy?

A. Yes, it is.

Q. Can you show us where on this map the transom would be?

A. [Points to bathroom door]. Above that door, right there.

Q. I'm showing you Exhibit 13. Do you recognize it?

A. Yes, I do. I took this picture. It's the door to the bathroom in my office. The picture is taken from inside the bathroom.

Q. Does this photograph accurately reflect the way the bathroom door and window above the door looked on June 30, YR-1?

A. Yes, it does.

Q. Does the transom open?

A. Yes, that black rod in the picture is the mechanism to open it. It's still in place because our office is an old 1920s townhouse modified for our purposes, so it has historical features. But, as you can see, it's closed.

Q. Could Carter have opened the window?

A. Not without us hearing it, no. The cleaners are the only ones who open it to clean, and it creaks really loudly when they do so. It is never propped open though, and it wasn't the morning I saw Lucy Madrid.

Q. But you did meet with Lucy Madrid the morning of the pageant, around 10 a.m.?

A. Er, yes.

Q. She was a coach for one of the contestants?

A. Yes.

Q. You exchanged a few words with her?

A. Yes.

Q. In your office?

A. Yes.

Q. And she did give you a shoebox?

A. Yes.

Q. There was money in that shoebox.

A. Nice try. That trick isn't going to work on me. There was no money in that shoebox. Look, I know it looks bad. But that's precisely why I kept the double doors to the office wide open. I didn't want anyone drawing improper conclusions from it.

Q. Okay, what did you say to Lucy Madrid?

A. I had asked Lucy Madrid to bring by a pair of diamond earrings she was storing for me, and she brought them over. As I was walking her to my office she said she also brought back some of the gifts I had sent her—a pair of Louboutin shoes and some Swarovski jewelry. When I asked why, she said the shoes didn't fit her, and she had some kind of allergic reaction to the jewelry. When we got to my office, I asked her for the box, which she then gave to me. And after I looked inside the box, I said, "Great, it's all here. Don't worry. I'll make it up to you."

Q. What were you promising to make up for?

A. Well, as a perk of having worked in the fashion industry, I get things like shoes, and clothes, jewelry, and handbags from designers. I don't have much use for them, so I often pass them along to my friends. Lucy is a good friend, so I'd sent her some stuff, including those shoes and the Swarovski jewelry. Except, obviously it didn't work out because the shoes didn't fit her and the jewelry gave her an allergic reaction. I felt really bad, so I told her I'd make up for it.

Q. What did you do with those items?

A. The shoes and the Swarovski jewelry? I sent them to someone else. No point in having them go to waste.

Q. Who did you send it to?

A. Taylor Hawkins.

Q. Why did you send it to Taylor Hawkins?

A. I had stored a few personal items in Hawkins's studio. And the box of stuff was just a thank you.

Q. You stored things in Hawkins's studio to hide stuff from your wife during your divorce, correct?

A. Okay, I'm not proud of it, but yes. It was just some artwork—paintings and sculptures worth a good chunk of money. Look, I cheated on my wife, Imogene. Once. In late YR-2. With Miss Olympia YR-3. But she threw herself at me, how could I say no? Imogene walked in, in the middle. And she swore she'd take every penny from me. She unleashed private detectives on me. I had to protect my assets somehow. So I liquidated some of my holdings, stored stuff at friends' places. You know the drill.

Q. Did you take anything out of the shoebox before you sent it to Taylor Hawkins?

A. Yes, the pair of diamond earrings that Lucy had been storing for me. The pair had belonged to my grandmother—I had to protect it during the divorce. It was not some kind of payoff.

Q. Why would Lucy Madrid be storing diamond earrings for you?

A. She was a friend.

Q. What did you do with those earrings?

A. I put them in the safe in my office.

Q. Was there any money in the shoebox?

A. No. Absolutely not.

Q. Was there any paper in that box?

A. Just some tissue paper the shoes were wrapped in. And a white envelope with the Swarovski jewelry in it.

Q. Was there a note in there that said "Thanks!"?

A. Honestly, this was so long ago, I don't remember clearly. Maybe. Or I think I may have scribbled it on a piece of white paper and put it in there for Taylor. I'm not sure.

Q. How did you have the package sent to Taylor Hawkins?

A. I asked Rory Carter to messenger it.

Q. Do you usually messenger such stuff?

A. No, I send it via UPS usually. But since there was jewelry in it, I thought I'd be safe. I even called Hawkins or maybe I had Carter call Hawkins to confirm that it was delivered.

Q. Did you personally talk to Hawkins to confirm it was delivered?

A. Yes, I did.

Q. How did you recognize Hawkins's voice?

A. Hawkins and I are really good friends—we have been for a long time. I recognize the voice well.

Q. What did you talk about?

A. I confirmed that Hawkins had received the package and said thank you for helping me out.

Q. Did you say anything else?

A. No.

Q. Did you use the phrase "we have a deal?"

A. What? No. There was no deal to have.

Q. Showing you Exhibit 10. Do you recognize it?

A. Yes, it's an email I wrote to Taylor Hawkins back on February 21, YR-1. It's accurate.

Q. In the first line, you ask Taylor to please email you about "this stuff" on your personal account. Why is that?

A. Like I said, I'm a very private person. I'm very particular about keeping personal and professional separate.

Q. In the next line though, you guarantee Taylor Hawkins a spot as the chief judge. Isn't that professional?

A. Yes, but most of the email is personal and it wasn't an official offer. That would come from the company.

Q. Is it your responsibility to find the pageant judges?

A. No, Gary Huxtable is in charge of that. But as the CEO, I had the final say.

Q. In the second to last paragraph of Exhibit 10, you discuss a package you sent Taylor Hawkins.

A. Yes, yes, clothes, shoes, that kind of thing.

Q. You also mention a deal. What deal are you referring to?

A. Oh, that's just our deal to let me store the valuables in Hawkins's studio. The arrangement I already told you about.

Q. I'm showing you what has been marked as Exhibit 6. Do you recognize it?

A. Yes, it's a deposit slip for some cash I had Carter deposit in my bank account.

Q. On the day of the pageant?

A. Well, yes. When Lucy Madrid brought me my grandma's earrings back, I opened up the safe to put the earrings in. I noticed the money in the safe. I closed out a savings account when the divorce proceedings began and put the cash in my safe. But since I was told by my lawyer that I had to pay my wife the monetary equivalent of half of my assets as part of our property settlement agreement, I figured there was no need to hide it anymore. I thought it would be better off in a bank, so I had Carter deposit it.

Q. Let's talk about the pageant. How did the YR-1 pageant go?

A. It wasn't our best showing, I'll be honest, but it wasn't terrible. The music cut out at one point, and the air conditioning at another point, but it was okay. The contestant whose music cut out, Miss Frenchtown, handled it beautifully. I'm sure the judges knew better than to penalize her for it.

Q. How many rehearsals did you have?

A. One complete run-through and other partial run-throughs. In retrospect, we could have benefitted from another full rehearsal, but we just didn't have the time.

Q. The pageant was short one judge. What happened to the fifth judge?

A. He had a car accident the morning of the pageant. He was in the hospital. Obviously, we couldn't help that. Although, Gary, the guy in charge of organizing the judges, really should have had a backup judge. Gary did an awful job. He should have been the one they fired. But no, they fire me instead.

Q. How did you decide to handle the scores?

A. We doubled the chief judge's score.

Q. Why not average it out?

A. Well, the average score would be very similar to the final score. That's just silly. Hawkins and I thought it best to double the chief judge's score instead.

Q. I'm handing you what has been marked as Exhibit 8. Do you recognize it?

A. Yes. It's the Master Scores Tally Spreadsheet for the YR-1 Miss Olympia Pageant. This is a spreadsheet that contains all the scores across all categories for the top ten contestants.

Q. Who created this document?

A. The scorekeeper creates it as each judge passes in his or her score sheet during the course of the pageant for each individual contestant in each category. It is created as a matter of business practice. We keep these spreadsheets every year for our records at our corporate office; we have them going all the way back to the first pageant.

Q. Who supervises the creation of the spreadsheets during the pageant?

A. An independent auditing company retained by Miss Olympia, Inc. supervises the creation of the spreadsheets. You know, like in the Oscars.

Q. And are the spreadsheets ever altered after the pageants have taken place?

A. No.

Q. Next, I'm showing you what has been marked as Exhibit 17. It's a video.

[Stanton watches video]

Q. Do you recognize it?

A. Yes, it's a video of the runner-up, Miss Scattersburg, answering her interview question.

Q. That was the contestant coached by Lucy Madrid, correct?

A. Yes, I believe it was.

Q. Would you agree that she didn't answer the interview question very well?

A. Well, okay, yes. I'll give that to you.

Q. Doesn't it surprise you that she was the runner-up of the competition?

A. It's surprising, yes, but that doesn't mean someone cheated. The results surprise me all the time. When I was at Beauterrific, we had this contestant who was wearing a two-piece gown for the evening gown competition—a leotard with a floor-length skirt over it, you know the types with the large slits? During her walk, she stepped on the skirt, and ripped it right off her body. She was standing there in a leotard. And they crowned her the winner. When I talked to the judges after that competition, they said they were very impressed by the way she handled the situation—it showed character. Can you believe it? Her evening gown was essentially a leotard, and she won. So, surprising means nothing.

Q. Did you have sexual relations with any employees at Miss Olympia?

A. No. Just Miss Olympia YR-3.

I, Harper Stanton, have read the above written transcription of the testimony I gave at my deposition on this 8th day of December, YR-1, and it is a true, accurate, and complete rendering of the testimony I gave.

Harper Stanton
Harper Stanton

UNITED STATES DISTRICT COURT
DISTRICT OF NITA

HARPER STANTON,	)	
	)	
Plaintiff,	)	
	)	
	)	
vs.	)	Case No: 00-CV-5120
	)	
	)	
TOBY ARMSTRONG,	)	
	)	
Defendant.	)	
	)	

DEPOSITION TESTIMONY

<u>TAYLOR HAWKINS</u>, having been first duly sworn, was examined and testified as follows:

EXAMINATION

<u>By ZACHERY ALLEN Attorney for the Defendant</u>:

Q. Please state your name for the record.

A. My name is Taylor Hawkins.

Q. Where do you live?

A. I live in Nita.

Q. How old are you?

A. I am fifty-three years old.

Q. Are you married?

A. Yes, I am.

Q. Did you go to college?

A. Yes, I did.

Q. What did you study?

A. I studied fashion design at the University of Nita.

Q. What did you do after you graduated from the University of Nita?

A. I worked for a fashion designer for a few years before I started my own finishing school for young adults about fifteen years ago—the Hawkins Finishing School.

Q. What is a finishing school?

A. It teaches young adults how to carry themselves in public. The curriculum focuses on manners, etiquette, professional dress, and public speaking.

Q. How did you become involved in the pageant industry?

A. The fashion designer I worked for was well known in the pageant industry and worked with many contestants. Later, when I started my own business, I provided training for pageant contestants. Eventually, I was approached by a pageant to be a judge. And I have been judging pageants for about the last three or four years with increasing frequency.

Q. Does your company still provide services to pageant contestants?

A. Yes, but once I started judging pageants, I was conflicted out of providing services to individual contestants who competed in competitions that I judged. So that decreased the number of individual contestants I work with. However, pageants sometimes hire my company to give all the contestants in the pageant an orientation on presentation, posture, and public speaking. Pageant management hires us to conduct this training so that the pageant will be of a high quality across all contestants.

Q. Why is that not a conflict of interest?

A. Because my company is helping all of the contestants equally.

Q. Has your company ever been retained to provide such training services by Miss Olympia, Inc.?

A. Yes. We have been providing such training services to Miss Olympia for the last four years.

Q. How much are you compensated for providing these training services to the Miss Olympia Pageant?

A. Not much at all. We charge about $100,000 for each presentation. You look surprised. But you have to understand that we are making a presentation to about fifty young women, and we need at least ten experienced staff members on hand during the presentation to help the contestants individually. And the presentation lasts an entire day. It is more of a workshop than presentation. It really improves the final product—the show on stage.

Q. How many such presentations do you make during the course of a pageant?

A. Usually just one a few days before the pageant. And we only do it for the big pageants. The smaller pageants don't have the money to pay for this kind of attention to detail.

Q. Do you see the pageant contestants individually then? Before the actual pageant?

A. No. When I am judging the pageant, I do not interact with the contestants before the pageant. My staff handles presentations at pageants where I am scheduled to judge.

Q. Does your staff ever discuss the pageant presentation sessions with you?

A. Not the particular contestants. They know to keep me out of it.

Q. How did your company come to provide training services for Miss Olympia, Inc.?

A. My company is well known in the industry for these training sessions.

Q. Did you approach Miss Olympia about providing the training sessions or did Miss Olympia reach out to you first?

A. I approached Miss Olympia about it. But after our first session, which was a hit, Miss Olympia called us back each year. Besides, once Stanton was at the helm, it was a no-brainer. Stanton has worked with us before and knows the quality of our work.

Q. How long have you judged Miss Olympia Pageants?

A. Miss Olympia gave me my first opportunity to be a judge back in YR-3.

Q. So, Stanton's first pageant at the helm of Miss Olympia?

A. Hmm, I didn't realize that. Yes, I guess so.

Q. How did Miss Olympia first approach you?

A. I knew Harper Stanton from my time as a fashion designer. Harper called me out of the blue one day and asked me if I wanted to be a judge.

Q. As a pageant judge, do you get paid for your services?

A. Yes. I am paid about $20,000 as the chief judge.

Q. You say as the chief judge, do the other judges get paid less?

A. Yes, I think they are paid about $10,000.

Q. Why is it that you make more money as the chief judge?

A. I do more. For example, if there is a tie, I have to break it. I am also a well-known name because of the Hawkins Finishing School, so I am worth more.

Q. I am handing you what has been pre-marked as Exhibit 10. Do you recognize it?

A. Yes. It is an email from Harper to me.

Q. Is it a fair and accurate copy?

A. Yes, it is.

Q. What is the email about?

A. I emailed Harper to find out if I was to be retained as a judge for the YR-1 Miss Olympia Pageant. I was having some scheduling difficulties and needed to know how to prioritize my commitments.

Q. The first line of the email asks you to send such correspondence to Stanton's personal account. Why is that?

A. I'm not sure actually. You'll have to ask Harper that.

Q. In the last line of the email, Stanton refers to a package. What was that package?

A. Harper sends me designer outfits from time to time. When you keep in touch with the fashion industry, from time to time designers send you outfits, or shoes, or jewelry. If Stanton doesn't want it, Stanton passes them along to friends, which includes me. I use them in my business.

Q. How many times have you received packages such as these from Stanton?

A. Two, maybe three times.

Q. How are these packages sent?

A. Usually USPS, UPS, that kind of stuff. Only once, I received a package by messenger.

Q. When did Stanton send you the package by messenger?

A. This year actually. The day of the YR-1 Miss Olympia Pageant.

Q. Why was that?

A. Well, it contained some shoes and crystal jewelry. You'll have to ask Stanton why, but maybe it was messengered because the jewelry was pricey.

Q. Do you have some sort of agreement with Stanton about when you will receive such packages?

A. No. They are sporadic and infrequent.

Q. Has anyone ever seen you open these packages?

A. I don't believe so. Who would?

Q. Is there also cash in these packages?

A. No. That's preposterous.

Q. Does Stanton provide you with these packages as a bribe? Perhaps in exchange for scoring certain contestants higher than others?

A. This again. Look, I can see why you'd think that from this email. There's a reference to this "deal." But that is just the way Stanton talks. Makes everything seem like some big secret. Believe me, there's no agreement or anything. The two are completely unrelated. They are just outfits or shoes or jewelry. Most of them are hideous anyway and aren't worth anything. Costs more to messenger it over.

Q. Okay, what is the deal that Stanton refers to in the email?

A. Oh, that. Look, it's not my place to say this, but Stanton recently went through a messy divorce. Stanton asked me to store some of the more valuable belongings in the company's studio. I told Stanton it made me uncomfortable. Stanton was always trying to make up for putting me in an awkward position. He'd buy me drinks and said I would get some packages with some really nice merchandise as a thank-you for storing the stuff.

Q. Is that why Stanton sent you jewelry?

A. No, the February package referred to in the email just had some designer outfits and shoes. The packet in June had jewelry. As a belated thank-you for letting Stanton store stuff in my studio, I suppose.

Q. Why do you say that? Did the package in June have a note in it?

A. Yes, now that you mention it. Just a blank piece of printer paper, folded over, and it said "Thanks!" in big handwritten letters.

Q. Did you recognize the handwriting?

A. Honestly, I didn't think about it. And I don't even remember what the handwriting looked like now.

Q. For this June package, do you have the note, the box, and the stuff that was in it?

A. No, sorry. The stuff is probably in use somewhere in my studio, but I tossed the box and the note once I took the stuff out. It was just trash at that point.

Q. So you let Stanton store things in your studio?

A. Uh, I'm not proud of it, but yes. Just for a couple of months. Then Stanton took the stuff back. In early June, I believe.

Q. Okay. Let's talk about the YR-1 Miss Olympia Pageant. When was the pageant?

A. June 30, YR-1.

Q. From a judging stand point, how did it go?

A. Pretty run of the mill. There were a few mix-ups. But nothing major.

Q. What type of mix-ups?

A. Well, for starters, one of the judges was a no-show. So we doubled my score.

Q. Doubled your score? Why not average the scores of the four judges?

A. Stanton and I discussed it, but we thought it was a better option to double my score. When you average the scores of the four judges to use as the score of the fifth judge and average it all out again, there isn't much difference between the score of the fifth judge and the overall average. That didn't make sense to us. So we decided against it.

Q. Were you and Stanton the only decision makers?

A. Yes, we were. CEO of the pageant and chief judge—it's expected.

Q. Does it happen often that a judge doesn't show up?

A. No, that's really rare. We all know how to keep our commitments. I'm not sure who the judge was or what happened there.

Q. Were there any other mix-ups?

A. Well, the music cut out once during a contestant's talent piece; Miss Frenchtown, I believe. But she was a really good sport about it. No harm, no foul. There were also some times when the music faded out and back in during the group presentation numbers, and the place got really hot by the second half of the show.

Q. Is that common?

A. It happens once in a while. You can't always control technology or facilities. There are several rehearsals done leading up to pageant day, but what happens, happens. Everyone has to learn to deal with the unexpected. In fact, that's part of what we do in our one-day training presentation. We throw unexpected things at the contestants and see how they deal with them.

Q. Were you aware that there was only one full rehearsal done for the YR-1 Miss Olympia Pageant prior to the final run?

A. Oh, that's surprising. You'd think. . . . But no, I'm sure it was unavoidable. It just happens sometimes.

Q. Let's talk about the contestants. Were you surprised at the contestants who made the top ten?

A. No.

Q. What about the top five?

A. That's a difficult question to answer. The scores of the judges are added together, and then averaged, for the final score, and it's an inherently subjective process. Surprises are a part of it. I don't know or care about what the other judges think when I am scoring a contestant. I try to be completely unbiased and impartial. It is always a bit of a surprise who makes it to the top group—the top five.

Q. Did you expect all five final contestants to make it to the top five?

A. Yes. I was not surprised by any of the top five in this pageant.

Q. And how about the pageant winner?

A. I expected her to win. She was great across all categories.

Q. What about the runner-up?

A. Well, her answer to the judge's question wasn't great, but she looked lovely and pulled her answer together by the end. She also scored highly in other areas.

Q. I'm showing you what has been pre-marked as Exhibit 17. It's a video clip. Do you recognize it?

A. Oh, yes. It's a clip of the runner-up's answer to the judge's question.

[Taylor Hawkins watches clip contained in Exhibit 17.]

Q. Is Exhibit 17 an accurate copy of the answer that the runner-up, Miss Scattersburg, gave at the YR-1 Miss Olympia Pageant?

A. Yes. That's exactly how it happened. Like I said, she gave a poor answer at the start but pulled it together at the end.

Q. I'm showing you what has been pre-marked as Exhibit 8. Do you recognize it?

A. It looks like the Master Scoring Spreadsheet. I haven't seen it before because the judges aren't supposed to see each other's scores, but my scores look accurate.

Q. Do the scores given by the other judges for any of the contestants surprise you?

A. Some of them look a bit low. But that's just my personal opinion. Like I said, the process, to a certain extent, is unpredictable.

Q. How are the contestants judged?

A. The judges are given judging criteria for each category. We score each contestant against the criteria.

Q. What do you mean by against the criteria?

A. We don't judge the contestants against each other. Instead, they are judged against the criteria. It is fair that way. Otherwise there would be no way to score the first contestant. You would have nothing to judge her against. So, under this system, it is possible to have all tens or all ones or anything in between. Each contestant is independently judged.

Q. What is a perfect score at the Miss Olympia Pageant?

A. A ten out of ten in all categories.

Q. How many categories are there?

A. There are four categories. All contestants compete in the bathing suit and evening gown categories. The field is then cut to ten. The top ten perform for the talent portion of the competition. The contestants are then cut to five. The top five are interviewed by the host and must answer a question of global interest.

Q. Can you recall what score you gave Miss Scattersburg in her final interview?

A. Yes. I gave her a nine.

Q. After watching that video contained in Exhibit 17, do you believe she deserved a nine?

A. It does seem a bit high. I remember laboring over this score. Yes, the first part of her answer to the question was poor, but she really pulled it together in the end. She finished strong and I think that overcame the rough beginning.

Q. I refer you back to Exhibit 8, the Master Scores Tally Spreadsheet. Please review the scores that the other judges gave Miss Scattersburg for her talent performance. Can you explain why your scores are so much higher than the other judges?

A. Like I said, I don't care about how the other judges score a contestant. I make my own independent assessment.

Q. Let's look at the Miss Scattersburg's scores for her talent performance. Would you agree with me that your scores are considerably higher than those of the other judges on Miss Scattersburg's talent performance?

A. Yes. I assume that the other judges marked her down for having an unconventional talent. She was juggling knives to a hip-hop song. But I marked her up for the flair and confidence with which she performed.

Q. Is it possible that the scores were fixed?

A. No.

Q. Why do you say no?

A. As the chief judge, I interact with the other judges. I can vouch for the judges and say we provide an entirely unbiased opinion. I saw nothing to suggest foul play. Our scores are unbiased, independent evaluations of the contestants. They are not tampered with in any way.

Q. Is there any way that Harper Stanton could have influenced the result?

A. None that I can think of.

Q. Did Harper Stanton influence your scores at the YR-1 Miss Olympia Pageant?

A. No.

Q. Have you been sued in connection with this scandal?

A. What scandal? There is no scandal. There was no bribe. No one fixes pageants. It's a silly rumor. And no, I have not been sued.

I, Taylor Hawkins, have read the above written transcription of the testimony I gave at my deposition on this 6th day of December, YR-1, and it is a true, accurate, and complete rendering of the testimony I gave.

/s/ Taylor Hawkins
Taylor Hawkins

UNITED STATES DISTRICT COURT
DISTRICT OF NITA

HARPER STANTON,	)))	
Plaintiff,	)))	
vs.	)))	Case No: 00-CV-5120
TOBY ARMSTRONG,	)))	
Defendant.	))	

DEPOSITION TESTIMONY

<u>TOBY ARMSTRONG</u>, having been first duly sworn, was examined and testified as follows:

EXAMINATION

<u>By MARGO JONES, Attorney for the Plaintiff</u>:

Q. Please state your name for the record.

A. My name is Toby Armstrong.

Q. Where do you live?

A. I live at 185 Beaumont Avenue, Nita.

Q. How old are you?

A. I am forty-two years old.

Q. Are you married?

A. I am divorced.

Q. Do you have any children?

A. I have a son.

Q. Did you go to college?

A. Yes, I did.

Q. What did you study?

A. I received a bachelor's degree in psychology. I also minored in journalism.

Q. What did you do after you graduated from the University of Nita?

A. I worked for Beauterrific, Inc.

Q. What does Beauterrific, Inc. do?

A. It is a beauty pageant management company. They assist pageants in planning, managing, and running beauty pageants.

Q. What was your role at Beauterrific?

A. I worked in various managerial positions in the company, and worked my way up to Pageant Event Manager.

Q. Do you still work at Beauterrific?

A. No. I left Beauterrific in YR-14 to raise my son. I judged beauty pageants on the side.

Q. What do you do now?

A. I own and run my own business—Pageant Stars Coaching Service.

Q. When did you start this business?

A. Back in YR-8.

Q. What does this business do?

A. We coach beauty pageant contestants in preparation for their pageants. We are a full-service organization—we provide everything from fitness and nutrition coaching, to interview training, to styling the contestant.

Q. Where is your business located?

A. 7210 Prometheus Circle, Suite 300, Nita City.

Q. How many contestants do you coach in a given year?

A. Between fifteen and thirty.

Q. Do you coach more than one contestant per pageant?

A. No. We have a strict policy against it. We want to be able to give each contestant 100 percent, without splitting our loyalties.

Q. What is your success rate?

A. In the last three years, we have had two contestants win their pageants; one was a runner-up, four placed in the top five, and eight placed in the top ten.

Q. Do you know Miss Olympia's former CEO—Harper Stanton?

A. I do.

Q. How do you know Stanton?

A. Well, I first met Stanton when I was at Beauterrific. Stanton was my direct supervisor, but we never really got along. I worked hard and expected recognition for my work, but Stanton was one of those people who took credit for other's work. Stanton always used to say it's "Harper's way or the highway." Our relationship reached a tipping point in YR-15 when Stanton passed me over for a promotion that I deserved. In fact, I remember confronting Stanton about the promotion. Stanton just smirked and said, "When you get in line, you can climb the ladder." I tried going over Stanton's head to bring up the issue with upper management, but somehow Stanton managed to make me look bad. Since then, I have had run-ins with Stanton when I was a judge, and now as a coach.

Q. What do you mean by run-ins?

A. Well, Stanton and I continued to butt heads every step of the way. We have never really found a way to get along. I can't get along with someone I don't respect—someone who truly deserves no respect.

Q. Changing gears somewhat, have you ever worked for Miss Olympia, Inc.?

A. No, I haven't.

Q. Have you ever applied for a job with Miss Olympia, Inc.?

A. Yes, twice.

Q. When was the first time?

A. Back in YR-4. Miss Olympia was looking to hire a Chief Executive Officer, and I was approached by a headhunter for the job.

Q. Did you apply for the position?

A. Yes, I did. But I didn't get it.

Q. I'm handing you what has been marked as Exhibit 12. Do you recognize it?

A. Yes, it's the rejection letter Miss Olympia sent me.

Q. Is it a fair and accurate copy?

A. Yes, it is.

Q. Do you know who Miss Olympia hired as CEO instead?

A. I found out soon enough. It hired Harper Stanton as its CEO.

Q. Did you two ever discuss Stanton's employment arrangement with Miss Olympia?

A. Please, there was no way Stanton would let me get away without bragging about the arrangement in detail. Somehow, Stanton found out I had also been interviewed for the job, so the next time we saw each other at the contestant audition, Stanton bragged about the contract terms—five-year contract for more than a million dollars, renewable. How humiliating. As if being rejected wasn't enough. Stanton really didn't deserve the job. It was only a matter of time until Stanton would get caught doing something inappropriate. I heard rumors that Stanton was cheating on the wife with the HR Director, Abigail Cotton. No big surprise. I'm sure Miss Olympia regrets hiring Stanton now.

Q. You said you applied to Miss Olympia twice. When was the second time?

A. In October of this year. As you may know, they are in the market for a new CEO.

Q. Has Miss Olympia made a hiring decision yet?

A. Not one that has been communicated to me. I only just interviewed with them two weeks ago.

Q. Did you have a contestant participate in the YR-1 Miss Olympia pageant this year?

A. Yes, I did. Miss Frenchtown.

Q. Did your contestant win?

A. No. My contestant made it to the top ten, but did not make it to the top five.

Q. Do you know why your contestant didn't make it to the top five?

A. They don't reveal that information. But I'll tell you, it was some nonsense. My contestant was fantastic. She deserved to win.

Q. Did you encounter any problems in the way the pageant was managed?

A. Yes, there were many problems. The pageant started over half an hour late. Then, the music cut out during my contestant's talent segment. Obviously, that appears to have been held against her. Not to mention there was one judge less than promised. The judge just didn't bother to show up. And rather than averaging the scores of the other judges for the score of the fifth judge, Stanton just doubled the score of the chief judge. Ridiculous and totally improper. First of all, what kind of pageant cannot get all its judges to show up on the final day? But worse yet, what pageant introduces bias into its scoring by doubling the scores of one of the judges?

Q. How did you react when you saw these issues?

A. I was embarrassed for them. Everything was a mess! I went to Twitter to rant about it.

Q. Was this before the blog post?

A. It was.

Q. I am showing you what has been marked as Exhibit 23. Do you recognize this document?

A. Yes. This is a copy of the tweets I sent out about the pageant.

Q. Does Exhibit 23 contain all of the tweets you sent out about the pageant on July 5, YR-1?

A. Yes.

Q. Were you aware that the absentee judge was rushed to the hospital the morning of the pageant as a result of a car accident?

A. That's too bad, but it doesn't change things. It is still the pageant's responsibility to have five judges show up to the event. Did they never think to appoint a back-up judge?

Q. How have your contestants fared in prior Miss Olympia Pageants?

A. In the last three years, since Stanton took over management, I have had none of my contestants win or make it to the top five. My contestant in the YR-1 Miss Olympia Pageant was my only top ten. Before that, in YR-6 and YR-5, my contestants made it to the top five. In fact, in YR-5, my contestant was the first runner-up.

Q. Let's talk about your blog. I'm handing you Exhibits 2, and 20, 21, and 22. Do you recognize them?

A. Yes, these are entries from my blog.

Q. Did you personally write these blog posts?

A. Yes.

Q. What is your blog about?

A. It's a tips and tricks blog, as well as just general news about the pageant world. I like to keep my readers informed. What potential contestants should know before they enter a beauty pageant.

Q. What is the name of your blog?

A. Pageant Tips.

Q. Is it a public website?

A. It was before this lawsuit. I've taken it down for the time being.

Q. Is your blog visited widely?

A. Yes, I would say so. I receive about 150 views a day, even more during pageant season.

Q. Do you run the blog yourself?

A. Yes, I do create my own posts. My blog is often featured on larger platforms, such as The Puffington Post and other pageant news websites.

Q. Let's discuss Exhibit 2. In it you make a pretty serious allegation. You allege that Stanton was bribed to rig the pageant in favor of at least one contestant, the first runner-up.

A. Yes. That's right.

Q. And you state that you got your information from an inside source?

A. Yes, I did.

Q. Who was your source?

A. Well, I guess, no harm done by telling you now. You already know. It's Rory Carter. I did not use the name originally to preserve anonymity of my source.

Q. How do you know Carter?

A. Just through the Miss Olympia Pageant. Carter was Stanton's personal aide, and since I attempted to avoid Stanton whenever possible, I ended up dealing with Carter much of the time.

Q. When did Carter come to you?

A. Shortly after witnessing the incident. The same day as the YR-1 pageant.

Q. What did Carter tell you?

A. That Carter had just witnessed an incident in which a coach had given Stanton some money in a shoebox.

Q. Is that inherently problematic?

A. Exchange of money generally? Not exactly. But if you put it all together. Cash from a coach, in a shoebox, and on the day of the pageant. Carter said the coach and Stanton were acting suspicious. Cash changed hands. And then that coach's contestant, who was a disaster by the way, not only makes it to the top five, but ends up as the runner-up. Yeah, I'd say it's problematic.

Q. Did Rory Carter tell you anything else about the incident?

A. Yes. Rory said Harper Stanton said to the coach, "Great, it looks like it's all here." And then maybe something about a deal of some sort. That nailed it down as a payoff for me.

Q. Did you report the allegations to anyone before the pageant started?

A. No. I didn't think it was my place. I thought I should wait to see what happened to the contestant coached by the briber before I told anyone anything. My suspicions were confirmed when the bribing contestant was the runner-up.

Q. Did you talk to the coach about it?

A. Yes.

Q. When did you talk to her?

A. Two days after the pageant.

Q. What is her name?

A. Lucy Madrid.

Q. What did she say when you spoke with her?

A. She denied everything. Acted completely flabbergasted, as if what I was saying was preposterous. Won't even talk to me now, which makes me think there really was something going on.

Q. Did you witness any part of the incident?

A. No.

Q. At the time when you published the blog post contained in Exhibit 2, did you know anything about Harper Stanton's relationship with Taylor Hawkins?

A. Yes, I knew that Taylor Hawkins was the chief judge for the YR-1 Miss Olympia Pageant and that Stanton and Hawkins appeared to be close friends.

Q. Why do you say they were close friends?

A. At industry events, I would always see them chatting and laughing together.

Q. Did you know anything about Stanton sending Hawkins packages?

A. No. So that's how Stanton did it.

Q. Did you confront Stanton about the incident?

A. What would have been the point?

Q. So you decided to blog about it?

A. Yes. It's important that Miss Olympia, Inc. know the truth. It's important that the world know the truth.

Q. Do you know how many times Exhibit 2 was read?

A. I have no idea.

Q. Did you approach Miss Olympia, Inc. officials with your allegations?

A. I encouraged Carter to approach them. I had no specific information about the incident other than what Carter told me—it made no sense for me to approach Miss Olympia, Inc. officials.

Q. What was your relationship with Carter like?

A. Strictly professional. Why do you ask?

Q. Well, did Carter ever approach you for a job?

A. Ah, yes, that. Carter applied for a job with Beauterrific in March of YR-1. Carter knew I had worked there and asked me for a letter of recommendation.

Q. Did you give Carter a letter of recommendation?

A. Not at that time, no. Carter was perfectly nice, but I hardly knew the kid. There wasn't much I could say in my letter of recommendation that would be worthwhile. So I politely declined.

Q. Did you ever write Carter a letter of recommendation?

A. Yes, in Aug—wait a minute. I see what you're doing here. I didn't offer Carter anything for this information on Stanton, if that's what you're thinking. Carter came to me voluntarily and gave me this information on Stanton's conduct.

Q. I'm handing you what's been marked as Exhibit 7. Do you recognize that?

A. Yes. It's the email I sent recommending Carter for a job at Beauterrific. Look, this was after the payoff to Stanton came to light. It had nothing to do with what Carter told me. Carter wanted a new job and there was absolutely no reason I shouldn't have helped.

I, Toby Armstrong, have read the above written transcription of the testimony I gave at my deposition on this 4th day of December, YR-1, and it is a true, accurate, and complete rendering of the testimony I gave.

Toby Armstrong

Toby Armstrong

UNITED STATES DISTRICT COURT
DISTRICT OF NITA

HARPER STANTON,	)	
	)	
Plaintiff,	)	
	)	
vs.	)	Case No: 00-CV-5120
	)	
	)	
TOBY ARMSTRONG,	)	
	)	
Defendant.	)	
	)	

DEPOSITION TESTIMONY

<u>RORY CARTER</u>, having been first duly sworn, was examined and testified as follows:

EXAMINATION

<u>By MARGO JONES, Attorney for the Plaintiff</u>:

Q. Please state your name for the record.

A. My name is Rory Carter.

Q. Where do you live?

A. I live in Frenchtown, Olympia.

Q. How old are you?

A. I am twenty-five years old.

Q. Are you married?

A. No, I'm not.

Q. Did you go to college?

A. Yes, I did.

Q. What did you study?

A. I studied business management at Olympia State University.

Q. What did you do after you graduated from Olympia State University?

A. I worked for Miss Olympia, Inc.

Q. What was your role at Miss Olympia, Inc.?

A. I was the CEO's personal aide. My official title was Senior Administrative Assistant.

Q. What did that role involve?

A. I helped with everything the CEO needed. For instance, from coordinating with vendors, organizing meetings, and briefing the CEO on important issues, to ordering lunch, dropping off packages at the post office, and keeping the CEO's calendar.

Q. Do you still work at Miss Olympia, Inc.?

A. No, I don't. I work at Beauterrific, Inc. now.

Q. How long have you worked at Beauterrific?

A. About three weeks.

Q. And what is your role at Beauterrific?

A. I am the Pageant Wardrobe Manager.

Q. What do you do as Pageant Wardrobe Manager?

A. I am essentially in charge of the contestants' collection of clothes for the pageant. I also oversee hair and makeup.

Q. Do you have employees reporting to you in this role?

A. Yes, I do. I have four employees reporting to me—one for hair, one for make-up, and two for wardrobe.

Q. Is there a substantial difference between the role you held at Miss Olympia and the role you hold at Beauterrific?

A. Absolutely. There is a difference in the level of responsibility. I have much more hands-on, direct, pageant-related managerial responsibility in my role at Beauterrific.

Q. Did you supervise any staff in your role as personal aide to the CEO at Miss Olympia?

A. No, I did not.

Q. Were you asked to leave Miss Olympia, Inc.?

A. No, absolutely not.

Q. Why did you leave Miss Olympia?

A. I just couldn't work for a company that does not value honesty and integrity. Besides, like I said, the job at Beauterrific has more responsibility. It's a better job. People work years before they get to supervise a team. It was just an opportunity I couldn't afford to pass up.

Q. Is the pay at Beauterrific greater as well?

A. Of course. It was a $10,000 pay raise.

Q. How did you get the job at Beauterrific?

A. I applied for it.

Q. Was this the first time that you applied for a job at Beauterrific?

A. Well, I had sent them my resume in response to a job posting in March, but I never heard from them.

Q. What was different this time around?

A. I think I was better suited for this role. The previous role I applied for was that of an office manager. It worked out for the best. This is the role I wanted to end up in anyway.

Q. Did anyone recommend you for your current position?

A. I think Toby Armstrong called or sent an email for me. I never reviewed it or confirmed that it actually happened. I assume it happened because Armstrong promised to do it.

Q. Was this the first time you asked Armstrong for a recommendation?

A. Well, I joked around with Armstrong back in March about a letter of recommendation, but it wasn't an official request. At the end of July YR-1, I heard there was another opening at Beauterrific, but I'm not sure who mentioned it to me. I talked to Toby about it, and Toby said, "I still keep in touch with people and could put in a word for you this time around." You could say Toby talked me into applying to Beauterrific again. So happy it worked out.

Q. Let's talk about your performance at Miss Olympia. What was it like?

A. I was a stellar employee. Harper Stanton saw potential in me right away. Stanton personally mentored and nurtured me.

Q. And how long did Stanton "personally nurture" you?

A. About a year and a half.

Q. And in this year and a half, is it fair to say that you spent quite some time with Stanton?

A. Yes, I was Stanton's personal aide, so I sat outside Stanton's office and we generally spent a lot of time together.

Q. I'm handing you what has been pre-marked as Exhibit 4. Do you recognize it?

A. Yes. It's my performance review for YR-2.

Q. What does it say?

A. What I already told you. That I was a stellar employee.

Q. On the second page how was your performance characterized?

A. Stanton said I was hardworking and diligent. Stanton also said I had great potential to be a leader in the company.

Q. I'm handing you what has been pre-marked Exhibit 5. Do you recognize it?

A. Yes. It's my performance review for YR-1.

Q. How would you characterize this review?

A. It is not very good. The HR Director, Abigail Cotton, reviewed me and said that my performance had fallen off.

Q. On the second page, under suggestions for improvement, it says approach internal management with problems and resolutions. What does that mean?

A. Just that I should be more communicative with management.

Q. Why do you think there was a drop in your performance?

A. There wasn't a drop in my performance. Cotton gave me a poor rating to get rid of me for telling Toby Armstrong what I saw in Stanton's office on the day of the YR-1 Pageant. I think she was just bitter that my actions ended her office fling with Stanton.

Q. What do you mean by office fling?

A. You know, she'd visit Stanton in the office frequently, and they'd be in there for half an hour with the door locked, and Stanton told me that they weren't to be disturbed. Even though nobody said it, we all knew what was going on. Once Stanton left Miss Olympia, Cotton rarely came by the office.

Q. In the year and a half that you worked with Stanton, have you ever witnessed Stanton do anything improper?

A. You mean other than cheating on a spouse and pageant-fixing? Nope, that's it.

Q. Let's talk about the pageant-fixing allegations you made. What did you witness on June 30, YR-1, the day of the YR-1 Pageant?

A. I clearly saw Stanton talking to one of the pageant contestant coaches. The coach was Lucy Madrid. Madrid was the coach for Miss Scattersburg in the YR-1 Miss Olympia Pageant and I had interacted with her before in my role as Stanton's assistant. Madrid gave Stanton a shoebox, and Stanton took it.

Q. A shoebox?

A. Yep, you know, one of those standard cardboard kinds that shoes come in.

Q. Where were you when you witnessed this?

A. Umm, in the bathroom.

Q. Were they in the bathroom too?

A. No, er, they were in Stanton's office.

Q. Where is the bathroom located?

A. It is inside Stanton's office.

Q. Is it Stanton's private bathroom?

A. Yes, it is.

Q. How were you able to observe the incident from Stanton's bathroom?

A. There's a window above the bathroom door, a transom—you know, that rectangular window you sometimes see above doors?

Q. How were you able to access that window?

A. I climbed up on the sink.

Q. It is a clear window?

A. It's mostly translucent, but there are clear stars in the middle that you can see through.

Q. Is that how you saw the exchange?

A. Don't remember exactly. Possibly. Actually, if I remember correctly, the window was propped open a couple of inches actually. Just enough for me to be able to look through it.

Q. I'm showing you Exhibit 13. Do you recognize it?

A. Yes, I do. It's a picture of the door to the bathroom in Stanton's office taken from inside the bathroom. That window above the door is what I looked through. And you see that black rod on the left? That opens the window and allows it to be propped open.

Q. Did you personally open the window?

A. No. I was surprised actually because I have never seen it propped open like that before. The cleaning staff usually opens it up to clean, and it makes this horrible, loud, screeching noise. If I had tried to open it then, Stanton and Madrid would surely have heard me. No, I assume the cleaning staff accidently left it open.

Q. Does this photograph accurately reflect the way the bathroom door and window above the door looked on June 30, YR-1?

A. Yes, it does except the window was open on that day and it isn't open in the photograph.

Q. And no one noticed you looking through the window?

A. Apparently not.

Q. Why didn't you just leave?

A. I . . . the public bathroom was occupied, so I used Stanton's bathroom. But once Stanton and the coach came in, I couldn't leave.

Q. Why not?

A. Nobody's allowed to use Stanton's private bathroom.

Q. Why did you look out instead of just waiting for them to leave?

A. I heard someone come in the office and I wanted to see who it was. I didn't want to get caught in the private bathroom, so I turned off the bathroom light and looked out the window.

Q. Okay. I'm showing you what has been marked as Exhibit 9. Do you recognize it?

A. Yes, it's a map of Stanton's office.

Q. Is it to scale?

A. For the most part.

Q. What is the double line on the right hand side of the map?

A. Those are the windows in his office.

Q. And the diagonal lines on the left hand side of the map?

A. Those are the double doors that open into his office.

Q. What is past those double doors?

A. My desk and a reception area with a couch, a few chairs, and a door to the main hallway.

Q. Was the door to the main hallway locked when you were in the bathroom?

A. No.

Q. When the coach and Stanton first came in, where were they standing?

A. From my perspective from the bathroom, the coach was standing on the left side of the desk near the door and Stanton was behind the desk. They were facing each other.

Q. Did they have any kind of conversation?

A. Not much. Stanton asked the coach, "Do you have it?" The coach gave Stanton the box and Stanton lifted the lid slightly, maybe three to four inches. Then Stanton said something like, "Great, it looks like it's all here. Don't worry. I'll take care of you." I heard the conversation clearly.

Q. How did you hear the conversation from the bathroom?

A. Like I said, the window was open. And they weren't whispering. In fact, they were somewhat loud.

Q. Did you see what was in the shoebox?

A. Yes, it looks like a stack of bills.

Q. Were you able to see it clearly?

A. Yes, I was. The coach handed Stanton the box over the corner of the desk. They were only about fifteen to twenty feet from the bathroom door when the exchange occurred.

Q. You would agree that you were looking at the exchange from above?

A. Yes, I was looking down. The window above the bathroom door is about seven feet off the ground.

Q. What was the lighting like in the room?

A. There was a lot of light streaming into the room from the windows. Plus Stanton's desk lamp is always on. And, from my vantage point, Stanton lifted the lid just enough so I could see pretty clearly what was in the box. It was paper. It looked like money.

Q. What did Stanton do with the box?

A. Well, after the coach left, Stanton closed the double doors to the office, then turned around to the bookcase and opened up the safe behind the books. It looked like Stanton took something out of the shoebox and put it in the safe. Then I couldn't see what was put in the safe because my view was blocked by Stanton's body. After that, Stanton took the shoebox and put it in one of those large padded envelopes and sealed it and left it on the desk.

Q. Around what time was this?

A. Approximately 10 a.m.

Q. Were you ever able to see who the envelope was addressed to?

A. Well, yeah. Later on that day, around 11:30 a.m., Stanton gave me that envelope and asked me to messenger it over to Taylor Hawkins, the chief judge in the pageant, and asked me to confirm with Hawkins when it had been delivered.

Q. Did you confirm that the package had been delivered?

A. Yes, I did.

Q. How did you confirm that?

A. Stanton asked me to get Taylor Hawkins on the phone.

Q. How did you know it was Taylor Hawkins on the line?

A. I called Taylor Hawkins' phone number, and Hawkins answered the phone saying, "This is Taylor Hawkins."

Q. What did they talk about?

A. Well, I transferred the call to Stanton, so I could only hear what Stanton said. First, Stanton asked, "Did you get it?" And then said, "Great, so we have a deal. See you tonight." And then hung up.

Q. How heavy was the package?

A. Heavier than a pair of shoes is what I thought at the time.

Q. Did you look inside the box when Stanton gave you the envelope?

A. No. How could I? It had already been sealed, and Stanton signed across the seal.

Q. Does Stanton messenger items and sign the seal frequently?

A. No. I've only seen it one other time. That was when Stanton asked me to messenger something over to one of the board members. About a year ago. That's it. Otherwise, we just use USPS or FedEx or something.

Q. Could it have been shoes?

A. Stanton claims the box had shoes and some jewelry in it. But neither of those things looks like a stack of paper now, does it? Besides, both of them, the coach and Stanton, appeared to be in a hurry and they looked really nervous and shifty. Looking around everywhere like they were making sure they were alone. Acting suspicious like they were doing something wrong. And here's the kicker, Stanton asked me to deposit $17,200 in cash into a personal bank account around 3 p.m. that same day. I mean, where else could the money have come from?

Q. Showing you what has been marked as Exhibit 6. Do you recognize that?

A. Yep, it's the deposit slip.

Q. Who filled out the form?

A. Stanton. All of the bright blue ink was written by Stanton. I recognize the handwriting.

Q. Have you ever deposited money for Stanton before?

A. Yes, I have. Both in Stanton's personal and business accounts. But it's never been more than a few thousand dollars. Maybe $3,000 maximum. Not nearly as much money as I deposited on that day.

Q. Did you confront Stanton about the transaction?

A. No, I did not. What would I even say? I saw you taking a bribe? Are you bribing the chief judge?

Q. Did you approach anyone in management about this alleged bribe?

A. No, it was the day of the pageant, and everyone was running around.

Q. Did you tell anyone about what you saw transpire between Harper Stanton and Lucy Madrid?

A. Yes. I told Toby Armstrong. I ran into Toby at the coffee shop near my office soon after I escaped from the bathroom. I was pretty distraught after seeing my boss take a bribe, so I talked to Armstrong about it.

Q. And how did Armstrong react?

A. Armstrong wasn't surprised. According to Armstrong, Stanton had done this at least once before—a few years ago when they worked at Beauterrific. Stanton had apparently rigged the entire pageant. When Armstrong tried to tell someone about it, nobody believed it. There was no concrete proof at the time, so nothing was done to Stanton.

Q. Did you tell Armstrong about the cash deposit and the shoebox?

A. No. I saw Armstrong before Stanton asked me to messenger the package to Hawkins and before the cash deposit. So I only told Armstrong about the exchange between Madrid and Stanton, and about what I thought I saw in the shoebox.

Q. Have you seen Stanton and Hawkins together?

A. Yes, they've been friends ever since I worked for Stanton. They have lunch together or talk on the phone at least once a month, if not more.

Q. One last question, have you been sued in connection with this incident?

A. No, thankfully.

I, Rory Carter, have read the above written transcription of the testimony I gave at my deposition on this 4th day of December, YR-1, and it is a true, accurate, and complete rendering of the testimony I gave.

Rory Carter

Rory Carter

UNITED STATES DISTRICT COURT
DISTRICT OF NITA

HARPER STANTON,	)	
	)	
Plaintiff,	)	
	)	
v.	)	Case No. 00-CV-5120
	)	
TOBY ARMSTRONG,	)	
	)	
Defendant.	)	
	)	

30(B)(6) DEPOSITION TESTIMONY OF ABIGAIL COTTON

<u>Abigail Cotton</u>, the designated representative of Miss Olympia, Inc. having been first duly sworn, was examined and testified as follows:

EXAMINATION

<u>By ZACHARY ALLEN, Attorney for the Defendant</u>:

Q. Please state your name for the record.

A. My name is Abigail Cotton.

Q. Where do you work, Ms. Cotton?

A. I work at Miss Olympia, Inc.

Q. What is your business's address?

A. 9800 Armante Road, Altamount, Olympia.

Q. I have marked as Exhibit 14 a notice of deposition to Miss Olympia, Inc. pursuant to Federal Rule of Civil Procedure 30(b)(6). Have you seen this document before?

A. Yes.

Q. Have you been designated by Miss Olympia, Inc. to testify on its behalf in response to this subpoena?

A. Yes, I have.

Q. And are you here to testify on all of the matters listed in this subpoena?

A. Yes, I am.

Q. What is your position at Miss Olympia, Inc.?

A. I am the Director of Human Resources.

[PAGES 2—5 HAVE BEEN OMITTED]

Q. I'm showing you what has been marked as Exhibit 12. Do you recognize it?

A. Yes, it's a Miss Olympia, Inc. rejection letter addressed to Toby Armstrong on July 23, YR-4.

Q. Was this copy of the rejection letter in your possession prior to the deposition today?

A. Yes, it was.

Q. And where was this letter kept?

A. In the Human Resources office for Miss Olympia, Inc.

Q. Is this letter sent out to every applicant of Miss Olympia, Inc. who is rejected for a position?

A. Yes. With every interview that does not result in an extension of an employment offer, our office sends the applicant a letter informing them of the decision, once it is signed by Mr. Pittman, the Chairman of the Board of Directors.

Q. How, specifically, are the letters generated?

A. Mr. Pittman, along with the Board of Directors, will interview the applicant and if the individual is not offered a position, Mr. Pittman will draft the rejection letter based on that interview.

He then signs it and sends it via interoffice mail to the Human Resources Department, and we sent it to the applicant, keeping a copy, of course.

Q. When are these letters generated?

A. As soon as the hiring decisions are made at the end of all the interviews.

Q. And these letters are created for a business purpose and kept in the regular course of business?

A. Yes.

Q. Would Mr. Pittman also be available for deposition?

A. Unfortunately, Mr. Pittman suffered a stroke and has recently died.

Q. Let's talk about Rory Carter. Do you recognize that name?

A. Yes. Rory was an employee of Miss Olympia, Inc. from December YR-3 to November YR-1.

Q. I'm showing you what has been marked as Exhibits 4 and 5. Do you recognize them?

A. Yes, they are Carter's Performance Evaluations for YR-2 and YR-1.

Q. Are these created for business purposes and kept in the regular course of business?

A. Yes, they are.

Q. Who performed the evaluations in YR-2 and YR-1?

A. Harper Stanton performed Carter's YR-2 review, and I performed Carter's YR-1 review. Human Resources routinely performs reviews in the absence of a supervisor.

Q. Switching gears to Harper Stanton. How long was Stanton an employee of the company?

A. The company hired Harper Stanton in July YR-4, pursuant to a five-year contract.

Q. Showing you what has been marked as Exhibit 1. Do you recognize it?

A. Yes. It is a copy of Harper Stanton's employment contract.

Q. And employment contracts are created for business purposes and kept in the ordinary course of business?

A. Yes.

Q. Did the company cancel its contract with Harper Stanton prior to the expiration of the given year term?

A. Yes, it did. However, as you can see, pursuant to the contract, paragraph xxi, we were within our rights to do so.

Q. Why, specifically, did the company fire Stanton?

A. The YR-1 Miss Olympia Pageant was managed poorly and nowhere near up to our standards. We run a beauty pageant. We expect our contestants to be flawless, and we, similarly, must stage a flawless pageant. Therefore, it was decided that there would be a parting of ways when Mr. Stanton failed to do so for the YR-1 Pageant.

Q. Showing you what has been marked as Exhibit 18. Do you recognize it?

[Cotton listens to audio recording]

A. Yes, that is the Chairman of our Board of Directors, Mr. Pittman, and local radio person, Janie Apple. Mr. Pittman gave an interview on the Altamont Radio News Show after the YR-1 Pageant.

Q. Is it a fair and accurate recording?

A. Yes, it is.

Q. Do you know when the show aired?

A. Yes. I heard the original airing on July 10, YR-1. I believe it was replayed a few times after Stanton was terminated in August YR-1.

Q. When did you terminate Stanton?

A. Stanton's termination was effective on August 2, YR-1.

I, Abigail Cotton, have read the above written transcription of the testimony I gave at my deposition on this 6th day of December YR-1, and it is a true, accurate, and complete rendering of the testimony I gave.

Abigail Cotton
Abigail Cotton, Director—HR

APPENDICES

DISTRICT OF NITA
APPLICABLE CASE LAW

In the District of Nita, courts have ruled that certain news outlets may use qualified privilege as a defense against claims of defamation. Qualified privilege refers to communications where the individual who creates allegedly defamatory statements are allowed to do so due to a qualification. That qualification typically extends to traditional news outlets. In *Slate Financial Associates v. Fox,* 698 Ni. 2d 113 (Nita Court of Appeals YR-1), the court ruled in favor of a defendant who was the founder and creator of a news blog with 400,000 views per month. The defendant was sued by a local politician for allegations of corruption in elections. The factors the court considered in their ruling were the blog was relied upon by the community, that the blog post was a matter of public concern, and that the defendant was a registered freelance journalist.

PRELIMINARY JURY INSTRUCTIONS

You have now been sworn as the jurors who will try this case. This is a civil case involving disputed claims between the parties. Those claims and other matters will be explained to you later. By your verdict, you will decide the disputed issues of fact. I will decide the questions of law that arise during the trial, and before you hear final arguments in this case and retire to deliberate at the close of the trial, I will instruct you on the law that you are to follow and apply in reaching your verdict. It is your responsibility to determine the facts and to apply the law to those facts. Thus, the function of jurors and the function of the judge are well defined, and they do not overlap. This is one of the fundamental principles of our system of justice.

Before proceeding further, it will be helpful for you to understand how a trial is conducted. In a few moments, the attorneys for the parties will have an opportunity to make opening statements, in which they may explain to you the issues in the case and summarize the facts that they expect the evidence will show. Following the opening statements, witnesses will be called to testify under oath. They will be examined and cross-examined by the attorneys.

Documents and other exhibits may also be received as evidence.

After all the evidence has been received, the attorneys will again have the opportunity to address you and to make their final arguments. The statements that the attorneys make now and the arguments that they later make are not to be considered by you either as evidence in the case or as your instruction on the law. Nevertheless, these statements and arguments are intended to help you properly understand the issues, the evidence, and the applicable law, so you should give them your close attention. Prior to the final arguments by the attorneys, I will instruct you on the law.

You should give careful attention to the testimony and other evidence as it is received and presented for your consideration, but you should not form or express any opinion about the case until you have received all the evidence, the arguments of the attorneys, and the instructions on the law from me. In other words, you should not form or express any opinion about the case until you retire to the jury room to consider your verdict.

The attorneys are trained in the rules of evidence and trial procedure, and it is their duty to make all objections they feel are proper. When a lawyer makes an objection, I will either overrule or sustain the objection. If I overruled an objection to a question, the witness will answer the question. If I sustain an objection, the witness will not answer, but you must not speculate on what might have happened or what the witness might have said had I permitted the witness to answer the question. You should not draw any inference from the question itself.

During the trial, it may be necessary for me to confer with the attorneys out of your hearing, talking about matters of law and other matters that require consideration by me alone. It is impossible for me to predict when such a conference may be required or how long it will last. When such conferences occur, they will be conducted so as to consume as little of your time as necessary for a fair and orderly trial of the case.

At this time, the attorneys for the parties will have an opportunity to make their opening statements.

FINAL JURY INSTRUCTIONS AND VERDICT FORM

Members of the jury, I shall now instruct you on the law that you must follow in reaching your verdict. It is your duty as jurors to decide the issues, and only those issues, that I submit for determination by your verdict. In reaching your verdict, you should consider and weigh the evidence, decide the disputed issues of fact, and apply the law on which I shall instruct you to the facts as you find them, from the evidence.

The evidence in this case consists of the sworn testimony of the witnesses, all exhibits received into evidence, and all facts that may be admitted or agreed to by the parties. In determining the facts, you may draw reasonable inferences from the evidence. You may make deductions and reach conclusions that reason and common sense lead you draw from the facts shown by the evidence in this case, but you should not speculate on any matters outside the evidence.

In determining the believability of any witness and the weight to be given the testimony of any witness, you may properly consider the demeanor of the witness while testifying; the frankness or lack of frankness of the witness; the intelligence of the witness; any interest the witness may have in the outcome of the case; the means and opportunity the witness had to know the facts about which the witness testified; the ability of the witness to remember the matters about which the witness testified; and the reasonableness of the testimony of the witness, considered in the light of all the evidence in the case and in light of your own experience and common sense.

The burden of proof in this case is a preponderance of the evidence. On any claim in which the burden of proof is by a preponderance of the evidence, the party who has the burden of proof must persuade you, with the evidence, that the claim is more probably true than not true. This means that the evidence that favors that party outweighs the opposing evidence. Plaintiff Stanton has the burden of proof in both defamation and tortious interference with contracts.

Defendant Armstrong has the burden of proof for any affirmative defenses.

The issues for your determination on the claims of the plaintiff are whether the defendant defamed the plaintiff when the defendant posted a blog entry on the website alleging the plaintiff was involved in pageant fixing, and whether the defendant, via this statement, tortiously interfered with the plaintiff's employment contract with Miss Olympia, Inc.

A.   Defamation

Defamation is a tort that involves the invasion of a person's reputation and good name. Plaintiff Stanton claims that Defendant Armstrong harmed him/her by making the following statements: "[S]teer clear of the Miss Olympia Pageant for now! An insider revealed that the runner-up made it as far as she did through a payoff to Miss Olympia's CEO. It explains how a contestant who can't answer a simple question could make it into the top five let alone end up as the runner-up. What a sham and a shame! With all the negative publicity the pageant got this year, hopefully Miss Olympia will terminate its contract with Harper Stanton and hire a new CEO!" To establish this claim, the plaintiff must prove all of the following:

1)   That the defendant made one or more of the above statements to persons other than the plaintiff;

2) That these people reasonably understood that the statements were about the plaintiff;

3) That because of the facts and circumstances known to the readers of the statements, they tended to injure the plaintiff in his/her occupation or to expose him/her to hatred, contempt, ridicule, or shame, or to discourage others from associating or dealing with him/her;

4) That the defendant failed to use reasonable care to determine the truth or falsity of the statements;

5) That the plaintiff suffered harm to his/her profession or occupation; and

6) That the statements were a substantial factor in causing the plaintiff's harm.

If even one of the above noted required elements is lacking, the plaintiffs' cause of action for defamation must fail.

Defamatory words are, by definition, words that tend to harm the reputation of another so as to lower the person in the estimation of the community, to deter others from associating or dealing with the person, or otherwise expose a person to contempt or ridicule. To be actionable, the words must be communicated or "published" to someone other than the plaintiff.

For Plaintiff Stanton to recover, Defendant Armstrong's statements must have been statements of fact, not opinion. A statement of fact is a statement that can be proved to be true or false. An opinion may be considered a statement of fact if the opinion suggests that facts exist.

In deciding the issue, you should consider whether the average reader would conclude from the language of the statement and its contest that the defendant was making a statement of fact.

The defendant has raised the affirmative defense of truth. The defendant bears the burden of proving this affirmative defense and must do so by a preponderance of the evidence. The defendant is not responsible for the plaintiff's harm, if any, if the defendant proves that the statements about the plaintiff were true.

Defendant Armstrong does not have to prove that the statements were true in every detail, so long as the statements were substantially true.

The defendant has also raised the affirmative defense of qualified privilege. The defendant bears the burden of proving his affirmative defense and must do so by a preponderance of the evidence. The defendant is not responsible for the plaintiff's harm, if any, if the defendant proves that his blog post is protected qualified privilege as outlined in the governing case law for the District of Nita. The statements from the blog post in question may qualify as qualified privilege if the defendant can prove all of the following:

1) The material has an affiliation with a traditional news outlet;

2) The material was created in observance of journalistic practices;

3) The material contains information that is a matter of public concern;

4) The material is relied upon by members of a community; and

5) The material relied on anonymous sources.

For purposes of this section, an issue is a matter of public concern if the issue was being debated publicly and if it had foreseeable and substantial ramifications for nonparticipants. A matter of public concern involves a public issue which is important to the general public, and invokes a substantial amount of independent and continuing public attention.

B.   Tortious Interference with Contract

Plaintiff Stanton claims that Defendant Armstrong intentionally interfered with his/her employment contract with Miss Olympia, Inc. To establish this claim, the plaintiff must prove all of the following:

1)   That there was a contract between the plaintiff and Miss Olympia, Inc.;

2)   That the defendant knew of the contract;

3)   That the defendant intended to disrupt the performance of this contract;

4)   That the defendant's conduct prevented performance or made performance more expensive or difficult;

5)   That the plaintiff was harmed; and

6)   That the defendant's conduct was a substantial factor in causing the plaintiff's harm.

If even one of the above noted required elements is lacking, the plaintiffs' cause of action for tortious interference with contracts must fail.

It is not enough that the defendant intended to perform the acts which caused the result—he/she must have intended to cause the result itself, that is, interference with the contract.

The defendant has asserted the affirmative defense of fair and reasonable conduct.

The defendant bears the burden of proving his affirmative defense and must do so by a preponderance of the evidence. The defendant is not responsible for the plaintiff's harm, if any, if the defendant's conduct was fair and reasonable under the circumstances. In considering whether the defendant's conduct was proper, you may consider the following factors:

1)   The nature of the defendant's conduct;

2)   The defendant's motive;

3)   The interests of the plaintiff with which the defendant's conduct interferes;

4)   The interests sought to be advanced by the defendant;

5)   The social interests in protecting the freedom of action of the defendant and the contractual interests of plaintiff; and

6)   The relations between the parties.

At this point in the trial, you, as jurors, will decide only if Defendant Armstrong defamed Plaintiff Stanton and/or tortiously interfered with the plaintiff's employment contract with Miss Olympia, Inc. You will first return a verdict on these issues. If you find that Armstrong defamed Stanton and/or tortiously interfered with Stanton's employment contract, you will hear additional argument from the attorneys and you will hear additional witnesses testify concerning the issue of damages.

Your verdict must be based on the evidence that has been received and the law on which I have instructed you. In reaching your verdict, you are not to be swayed from the performance of your duty by prejudice, sympathy, or any other sentiment for or against any party.

When you retire to the jury room, you should select one of your members to act as foreperson, to preside over your deliberations, and to sign your verdict. Your verdict must be unanimous, that is, your verdict must be agreed to by each of you. You will be given a verdict form, which I shall now read and explain to you.

(READ VERDICT FORM)

When you have agreed on your verdict, the foreperson, acting for the jury, should date and sign the verdict form and return it to the courtroom. You may now retire to consider your verdict.

UNITED STATES DISTRICT COURT
DISTRICT OF NITA

HARPER STANTON,   )
)
Plaintiff,   )
)
vs.   )   Case No: 00-CV-5120
)
TOBY ARMSTRONG,   )
)
Defendant.   )
)

VERDICT FORM

We, the jury, return the following verdict:

1. Did Defendant Armstrong's July 5th, YR-1, blog post on Pageant Tips Blog alleging the YR-1 Miss Olympia pageant was fixed by a coach bribing the CEO of the pageant defame Plaintiff Stanton?

    YES _____   NO _____

2. Were Defendant Armstrong's statements made on Pageant Tips Blog on July 5, YR-1, substantially true?

    YES _____   NO _____

3. Did Defendant Armstrong tortiously interfere with Plaintiff Stanton's employment contract with Miss Olympia, Inc.?

    YES _____   NO _____

4. Was Defendant Armstrong's conduct in publishing the blog post alleging the pageant was fixed by paying a bribe to the CEO fair and reasonable under the circumstances?

    YES _____   NO _____

SO SAY WE ALL this _____ day of _____, YR-0.

Foreperson